ENGLISH GRAMMAR
for learners

LAROUSSE

Produced by

LAROUSSE LANGUAGE REFERENCE

General Editor

SCOTT FORBES

Editors

NICHOLAS JONES

MICHAEL MAYOR

TOM STABLEFORD

Consultants

TOM STABLEFORD

FAYE CARNEY

Design and DTP layout

SCOTT FORBES

CALLUM BRINES

© Larousse, 1993

ISBN 2-03-406003-2

Introduction

The LAROUSSE ENGLISH GRAMMAR is designed for students of English from intermediate to advanced level. Written by experienced teachers of English as a Foreign Language, it gives a concise outline of English grammar in an attractive and easy-to-use format. The key points are explained in simple language and fully illustrated with examples from everyday English.

Areas that cause special difficulty for the foreign learner are highlighted in note form (look for the headings **Compare** and **Note**). The same headings give extra information on pronunciation, register and American English.

At the end of the book you will find three sections designed for quick reference: a glossary of technical terms, a guide to the relationship between spelling and pronunciation, and a full index.

The layout of the book has been designed to help you to find the information you need quickly and easily. The main chapters (e.g. **Nouns**) are laid out in clearly numbered sections (e.g. **1. Nouns and their Plurals**) and sub-sections (e.g. **1.1 Regular plurals**). In addition there are numerous cross-references which allow you to explore a topic further. Note that these either refer you to another chapter and section (e.g. ⇨ **Verbs 1, 2.1**), or, if no chapter heading is given, to another section of the chapter you are already in (e.g. ⇨ **4.1**).

We are confident that the LAROUSSE ENGLISH GRAMMAR, with its practical approach and rich illustration of everyday usage, will prove an invaluable aid to revision and self-tuition.

Contents

Contents

Phonetic Alphabet

English Vowels

[ɪ]	pit, big, rid
[e]	pet, tend
[æ]	pat, bag, mad
[ʌ]	come, cut
[ɒ]	pot, log
[ʊ]	could, full
[ə]	mother, suppose
[iː]	bean, weed
[ɑː]	barn, car, laugh
[ɔː]	born, lawn
[uː]	loop, loose
[ɜː]	burn, learn, bird

English Diphthongs

[eɪ]	bay, late, great
[aɪ]	buy, light, aisle
[ɔɪ]	boy, foil
[əʊ]	no, road, blow
[aʊ]	now, shout, town
[ɪə]	peer, fierce, idea
[eə]	pair, bear, share
[ʊə]	poor, sure, tour

Semi-vowels

[j]	you, spaniel
[w]	wet, why, twin

Consonants

[p]	pop, people
[b]	bottle, bib
[t]	train, tip
[d]	dog, did
[k]	come, kitchen
[g]	gag, great
[tʃ]	chain, wretched
[dʒ]	jig, fridge
[f]	fib, physical
[v]	vine, livid
[θ]	think, fifth
[ð]	this, with
[s]	seal, peace
[z]	zip, his
[ʃ]	sheep, machine
[ʒ]	usual, measure
[h]	how, perhaps
[m]	metal, comb
[n]	night, dinner
[ŋ]	sung, parking
[l]	little, help
[r]	right, carry

The symbol ['] indicates that the following symbol carries primary stress.

The symbol [ʳ] indicates that the final 'r' is pronounced only when followed by a word beginning with a vowel. Note that it is nearly always pronounced in American English.

Nouns

1. Nouns and their Plurals

1.1 Regular plurals

■ Only countable nouns (⇨ **2.1**) have plurals.

■ The majority of English plurals are formed by adding -s:
book–books ▴ bird–birds ▴ hat–hats ▴ bag–bags

■ However, nouns ending in -s, -sh, -ch and -x, and some nouns ending in -o, take an -es ending in the plural:
bus–buses ▴ box–boxes ▴ kiss–kisses ▴ tomato–tomatoes

■ Nouns ending in a consonant + -y have plurals ending in -ies:
baby–babies ▴ cherry–cherries ▴ entry–entries
When there is a vowel before the -y the spelling is regular:
boy–boys ▴ valley–valleys

■ Nouns ending in -f or -fe have plurals ending in -ves:
wife–wives ▴ knife–knives ▴ half–halves ▴ leaf–leaves
Among the exceptions are belief, chief, cliff, proof, roof, safe. These words take -s in the plural.

To sum up:

Singular ending	Plural ending
-s, -sh, -ch, -x, (-o)	-es
consonant + y	-ies
vowel + y	-s
-f, -fe	-ves

Nouns ending in the sounds [f, k, p, t, θ] add [-s]:
  laughs, cakes, ships, hats, months
Nouns ending in [b, d, ð, g, l, m, n, ŋ, v], and all vowels, add [z]:
  jobs, birds, lathes, bags, bills, farms, sons, kings, gloves;
  boys, pianos, screws, teachers
Nouns ending in [dʒ, s, ʃ, tʃ, z, ʒ] add [ɪz].
  bridges, kisses, boxes, dishes, coaches, roses, garages
House [haʊs] has the plural houses ['haʊzɪz].
Path [pɑ:θ] has the plural paths [pɑ:ðz].

1.2 Irregular plurals

True Exceptions

In these cases, note the vowel changes:
  man–men ▲ woman–women ▲ child–children ▲ foot–feet
  tooth–teeth ▲ goose–geese ▲ mouse–mice ▲ louse–lice

Zero Plural

■ Some nouns are the same in both singular and plural. They
include:
  sheep, deer, fish, salmon, aircraft, series, species

■ Some number and measurement nouns have regular plurals when
used alone but often have zero plurals after numbers. They include
hundred, thousand; pound (money or weight), ton, foot:
  I have thousands of books. I've just bought *two hundred* more.
  He's *six foot* (or *feet*) tall and weighs *fourteen stone*.

■ Some foreign words, especially from Greek and Latin, can keep
their foreign plural. This is usually optional. Among those that
usually retain their foreign plurals in English are:
  basis–bases ▲ analysis–analyses ▲ thesis–theses

1.3 Nouns which are always plural

English has many nouns that are always plural. These may or may
not end with -s but always take a plural verb. They include:
  outskirts, cattle, police, trousers, scissors, clothes, thanks
  The *police have* arrested him.
  Whose *glasses are* those? They're mine.

1.4 Singular nouns ending in -s

An -s ending does not necessarily mean that a noun is plural. Some
nouns ending in -s are uncountable singular (⇨ **2.2**), e.g.
  news, mathematics, measles, billiards, the United States
  The *news is* bad.
  The *United States is* a very big country.

1.5 Group nouns

Nouns for groups of people or animals, such as **government**, **team**, **school**, can be either singular or plural. The choice depends on whether you are thinking of the group as a whole or as a set of individual people or things.

> **The government *has* made up its mind.**
> **The government *have* made up their minds.**
> **France *is/are* winning 2-0.**
> ***Do/does* your family still live in Kent?**

― Note ―

Having a verb in the plural form after a singular noun (as in the second example above) is more common in British English than in American English.

1.6 Plural nouns with singular verbs

When nouns for periods of time, sums of money and distances are used with a number, they take a singular verb:

> **Three weeks *is* a long time for a holiday.**
> **Five miles *is* too far to walk.**

2. Countable and Uncountable Nouns

> I want a sandwich.
> I want two sandwiches.
> I want some food.

There are two classes of English nouns:

2.1 Countable nouns

– are individual things we can count
– have a singular form and a plural form
– can be preceded by a number or **a/an**, or by **some** (if the noun is plural):

> **sandwich, child, chair, loaf, inch, idea, wish, view**
>
> I want *a sandwich*.
> I want *two sandwiches*.
> I want *some sandwiches*.

2.2 Uncountable nouns

– are 'masses' or substances, or abstract ideas
– do not have plural forms
– cannot be preceded by the indefinite article (**a/an**) or a number but can be preceded by **some**:

> **water, furniture, bread, money, dirt, weather**
>
> I want *some food*.
> I need *some money*.
> We want *peace*.

■ Whether a noun is countable singular, countable plural, or uncountable decides which determiners can be used before it and which pronouns can be used to replace it (➪ **PRONOUNS AND DETERMINERS**).

2.3 Countable v. uncountable nouns

■ Nouns which are usually countable can often be used uncountably. This usually changes their meaning and function.

> **He keeps *chickens* in his garden.** (= the birds)
> **Are we having *chicken* for lunch?** (= the meat)

Similarly, nouns which are usually uncountable can often be used countably. Often the countable form is used to mean a portion of the substance or thing.

> **Can I have *two cups of tea*, please?**
> **Can I have *two teas*, please?**

Compare

••

Two forms of the same word may have very different meanings.
Compare the following pairs:

Countable:
  Our house has eight *rooms*.
Uncountable:
  There's no *room* in the car for the dog.

Countable:
  We've been to Italy five *times*.
Uncountable:
  ***Time* is a great healer.**

••

2.4 Counting with uncountable nouns

Uncountable nouns, and nouns that are always plural (⇨ **1.3**),
cannot be counted in the usual way. To talk about certain amounts
of them, a phrase using a countable noun must be used.

■ Many uncountables can be counted by using piece or bit:

She gave me $\left\{ \begin{array}{l} \text{a piece} \\ \text{two pieces} \\ \text{a bit} \end{array} \right\}$ **of** $\left\{ \begin{array}{l} \text{news} \\ \text{work} \\ \text{cake} \end{array} \right\}$

Some phrases, however, are fixed and have to be learned
individually:
  an item of furniture
  a slice of bread/cake ▴ a loaf of bread ▴ a bowl of soup
  a spell of bad weather
  a packet of soap powder

■ Precise amounts can be referred to with measurement words:
  a gallon of petrol ▴ an ounce of tobacco

■ Plural nouns that are thought of as having two parts are used with
the phrase a pair of:
  a pair of trousers/scissors/glasses

▶ Note that the verb is singular with a pair but plural with the noun
itself:
  This pair of shorts *belongs* to Jim.
  These shorts *belong* to Jim.

■ Other plural nouns are counted using other countable nouns.
Again these combinations have to be learned individually:
  two sets of clothes ▴ a flight of stairs ▴ a group of people

3. The Possessive

■ The possessive form typically indicates ownership:
   Mary's suitcase

But it can also indicate some more general connection:
   women's studies (= studies for or about women)

■ The possessor is usually a person, group of people (e.g. **company,
team**) or animal, but words denoting things can also be possessive:
   the tree's branches ⌐ life's little pleasures

3.1 Forms

■ Singular nouns, and plurals which do not end in -s:
   NOUN + **-'s**
   **cat's, wife's, girl's, boy's, boss's, women's, James's
   a child's toy ⌐ children's toys**

■ Regular plurals already ending in -s:
   NOUN + **-'**
   cats', wives', girls', boys', bosses'

Compare

•••

   my sister's friend (= one sister)
   my sisters' friend (= more than one sister)

•••

> The rules for the pronunciation of the possessive forms [-s], [-z],
> and [-ɪz] are the same as for the pronunciation of regular English
> plurals (⟡ **1.1**), except:
> – words ending in [-f] or [-θ] keep this sound in the possessive and
> add [-s]
>   **wife's** [waɪfs]
> – personal names ending in [-s] or [-z] usually add [-ɪz] as expected
>   **the Jones's** ['dʒəʊnzɪz] **house**
> – plural nouns which already end in an [-s] sound do not change
>   **the United States** [juːnaɪtɪd 'steɪts]
>   **the United States'** [juːnaɪtɪd 'steɪts] **Senate**

3.2 Usage

■ Possessive nouns (with their determiners) go before the noun
referring to the thing possessed:
   our uncles' houses = the houses of our uncles

■ Possessive nouns are often used alone after the verb **be**:
   'That car over there, is it *your father's*?' 'No, it's mine.'

They are also used alone when -'s stands for **shop** or **house**:

We bought some sausages at *the butcher's*. (= the butcher's shop)
I heard the news at *Steve's*. (= Steve's house)

■ Phrases can contain more than one possessive noun:
Have you met *Jack's sister's* teacher?
(= the teacher of the sister of Jack)

■ Whole phrases can be made possessive. The -s is joined only to the final noun:
We visited the *King of Spain's* palace.
***Alice and Tracey's* mother has had an accident.**

■ The possessive is also used in certain other ways, for example to specify a period of time:
We're going to take *a week's holiday* at Easter.
I've just done *two days' hard work*.
(*NOT* **I've just done *a* two day's hard work.**)

▶ But note that this does not work for distance. We cannot say:
It's *four miles' walk* to the shop.
Instead we have to say:
It's *a four-mile walk* to the shop.

3.3 The -'s possessive v. the *of* possessive

■ An -'s possessive sometimes means the same as a phrase starting with of:
the company's profits = the profits of the company

However with personal names, only the -'s possessive is possible:
Bill's clothes

The 'of' form is more common when referring to objects:
the front of the house ▲ the corner of the room

It is also used in longer constructions:
I know the son of the writer you met at that party.
(*rather than* **I know the writer you met at that party's son.**)

Compare

●●●

■ In some cases the -'s possessive and the of possessive have different meanings:
my aunt's paintings = the paintings owned or painted by my aunt
the paintings of my aunt = the paintings showing my aunt

■ The -'s possessive usually includes the idea of the. A double possessive is used to show that the thing owned is *not* unique:
my father's friend = a particular friend
a friend of my father's = one of my father's friends

●●●

4. Compound Nouns

4.1 Forms

> a postman ▲ a furniture shop
> a mother-in-law ▲ a woman doctor

■ Nouns are often placed before other nouns to modify their meaning. The first noun is known as a *noun modifier;* the second noun is known as a *head noun:*

> a railway station ▲ a computer system ▲ a fashion model

■ Two nouns used together frequently are often thought of, and written as, a single noun. But this is not always the case:

> a postman *BUT* a post office
> a teacup *BUT* a coffee cup

Compare

●●

> a teacup (= a cup made to drink tea from)
> a cup of tea (= a cup that is full of tea)

●●

■ Noun modifiers before head nouns are usually in the singular. This is true even of words that do not usually have a singular form:

> a trouser press ▲ a scissor movement

But this is not always true, e.g. our sales floor, an arms dealer.

■ The modifying noun can itself be modified by another noun or an adjective. Hyphens are often used to show which words go together:

> a hot-water tap
> an all-seater football stadium
> a mail-order catalogue
> a French-government foreign-affairs spokesman

4.2 Plurals

■ Most compound nouns form their plurals in the regular way (⇨ 1.1) by making the second noun plural:

> express trains ▲ Easter eggs ▲ boyfriends ▲ grown-ups

■ The exceptions form their plurals as follows:

– When the last part of a compound noun is not itself a noun or is uncountable, it is often the first part that is made plural:

> passers-by ▲ fathers-in-law ▲ ladies-in-waiting

– A few compounds have two possible plurals:

> two spoonfuls *OR* two spoonsful

– Some others have 'double plurals'. They denote professions and are made up of two nouns, each of which describes the person concerned:

women doctors ▲ menservants

5. Word Formation

■ In English, it is possible to add elements to the beginnings and endings of words in order to change their meaning or grammatical class. Some common *prefixes* (added to the beginnings of words) and *suffixes* (added to the endings of words) are given below.

5.1 Prefixes

– used to form negatives:

de-	populate → depopulate
dis-	honest → dishonest
il-	legal → illegal
im-	possible → impossible
in-	tolerable → intolerable
ir-	regular → irregular
non-	fiction → nonfiction
un-	stable → unstable

– used to say something about time:

ante-, pre-	before
post-	after

– used to say something about nationality:

Afro-	African
Anglo-	English
Austro-	Austrian
Euro-	European
Franco-	French
Sino-	Chinese

– used to say something about number or quantity:

bi-	two
centi-	hundred
deca-	ten
deci-	ten
demi-	half
kilo-	thousand
mono-	one
multi-	many
poly-	many
semi-	half
tri-	three

5.2 Suffixes

– used to change the grammatical class of a word:

-ation	[verb → noun]	frustrate → frustration
-er	[verb → noun]	teach → teacher
-ify	[noun → verb]	simple → simplify
-ly	[adjective → adverb]	easy → easily
-ment	[verb → noun]	assess → assessment
-ness	[adjective → noun]	happy → happiness

– used to form comparatives/superlatives:

-er/-est	small → smaller → smallest

– used to form feminine nouns:

-ess	lion → lioness
-ette	usher → usherette

– used to say something about size:

-ette	kitchen → kitchenette
-let	drop → droplet
-ling	duck → duckling

– used to form related words:

-aholic	work → workaholic	(somebody who works a lot)
-ee	employ → employee	(somebody who is employed)
-free	lead → leadfree	(containing no lead)
-friendly	user → user-friendly	(kind to the user)
-ish	green → greenish	(slightly green)
-less	finger → fingerless	(without fingers)
-like	lady → ladylike	(like a lady)
-proof	flame → flameproof	(able to withstand flames)
-wards	home → homewards	(towards home)

Pronouns and Determiners

1. Personal Pronouns
I/me ▴ she/her ▴ they/them etc

2. Possessive Determiners and Pronouns
my/mine ▴ her/hers ▴ their/theirs etc

3. Reflexive Pronouns
myself, herself, themselves etc

4. The Indefinite and Definite Articles
the chair ▴ a chair ▴ the sun ▴ work

5. Numbers, One and Other
two ▴ the second
I'll take these two and you can have the other ones.

6. Quantifiers
some chairs ▴ any chairs ▴ a few chairs
much money ▴ many chairs ▴ no chairs

7. Indefinite Pronouns
somebody, everyone, no one, nothing

8. Demonstratives
this/that chair ▴ these/those chairs

9. Question Words
who?, what?, which?, where?, why?, how?

10. Relative Pronouns
the idiot who/that broke my pen

Determiners	Pronouns
The priest plays football.	*He* plays football.
This work is boring.	*This* is boring.
Give me *some* paper.	Give me *some*.
	Give me *something*.
I bought *the other* shirts.	I bought *the others*.

Determiners are used before nouns (and any adjectives and nouns that go with the nouns), and say something about which thing or person is being referred to. They include the articles (a and the), possessive adjectives (my, your, etc), demonstratives (this, that, etc), quantifiers (some, any, etc) and numbers.

Pronouns are used in places where you might otherwise find a noun, for example as the subject or object of a verb or after a preposition. They can be demonstrative (this, that, etc), indefinite (some, any, etc), interrogative (who, what, etc), personal (I, you, etc) or relative (who, that, etc).

■ Many determiners and pronouns have the same form, e.g. **this**, **some**. In other cases there are minor differences, e.g. the determiners **my** and **no** correspond to the pronouns **mine** and **none**. Some words can only be one or the other, e.g. **the** is only a determiner, **she** is only a pronoun.

■ The choice of pronoun or determiner depends on the type of nouns – countable singular, countable plural, or uncountable (⇨ **NOUNS, 2.**).

■ Note that shared determiners do not need to be repeated in lists:
   My uncle and aunt are coming.

1. Personal Pronouns

1.1 Forms

	Subject	*Object*
Singular		
1st person	I	me
2nd person	you	you
3rd person		
– *masculine*	he	him
– *feminine*	she	her
– *general*	one	one
– *with things*		it
Plural		
1st person	we	us
2nd person	you	you
3rd person	they	them

1.2 Usage

■ Nouns in English have no gender and both the indefinite article (a, an) and the definite article (the) are invariable (⇨ **4.**). The actual gender of the person or thing referred to is however reflected in the choice of personal and reflexive pronouns (⇨ **1. & 3.**).

   he is used for male humans and animals
   she is used for female humans and animals
   it is used for sexless things
   There's my brother. *He*'s a postman.
   There's my sister. *She*'s a driver.
   There's my car. *It*'s a Ford.

■ Numerous nouns can be either male or female e.g. doctor, cousin, friend, cyclist, shop assistant, or cat. The choice between he and she etc depends on what sex the person (or animal) really is:

There's my boss. Do you know *him/her*?
Have you met my dog? *He/She* doesn't bite very often.

Note

If necessary, the sex of neutral noun professions can be specified by adding woman/female or male:

nurse → male nurse ▴ doctor → woman doctor

The suffix -person is used to avoid referring to the sex of a particular profession:

chairman → chairwoman → chairperson
spokesman → spokeswoman → spokesperson

The suffix -ess can be used to create the feminine form:

manager → manageress ▴ author → authoress

However in current English usage, these may be considered pejorative.

■ With animal words, and a few human words including baby, it can be used if you do not know the actual sex:

Listen to that baby. I wish *it* would be quiet.

■ She is sometimes used to talk about countries and ships:

**The Titanic was thought to be unsinkable, but *she*
sank on her maiden voyage.**

Note

When the sex of a person is unknown:
Older formal usage uses the masculine pronoun.

If an employee is off sick, *he* must get a note from his doctor.

Modern formal usage uses masculine *and* feminine pronouns.

A teacher should always try to help *his or her* students.

Informal usage prefers they, them, their.

Everybody will get *their* wages on Monday.
It isn't easy living with an invalid when *they* can't look after themselves.

■ You, your, yours are both singular and plural, and are used regardless of how well you know the people you are speaking to.

■ Singular nouns referring to groups of people, for instance sports teams or business companies, are often treated as plurals. They are thus often replaced by they, etc (⇨ **Nouns, 1.5**):

Liverpool have sacked *their* manager.
The union say that *they* will go on strike.

> **Note**
>
> You is also used, especially in spoken English, to mean 'people in general' – for instance when asking for and giving instructions.
> '**How do *you* get to the station?**'
> '***You* go down here and take the second turning on the left.**'
> **They say the weather will be fine, but *you* can never be sure.**
>
> In more formal language, the general pronoun one (possessive one's) can be used in this sense. But its use is strictly limited and often sounds either foreign or affected.
> **The climate becomes drier as *one* moves east.**

1.3 Subject v. object

■ Subject pronouns are used when the pronoun is the subject of a verb:

Last night *I* saw someone *I* hadn't seen for years.
How many tickets are *we* going to buy?

When the subject includes I and others, the I is placed last:

My sister and *I* went to the same school.

■ Object pronouns are used:
– when the pronoun is the object of a verb. (There is no difference between direct objects and indirect objects.):

Does Alistair know *them* very well?
They gave you dinner. Did you thank *them* for it?

– after prepositions:

Chris will be staying with *us*.
You need to speak to someone like *him*.

> **Note**
>
> After the verb be, after words like **than** and **as**, and where the pronoun stands alone, formal English uses subject pronouns, even when the following verb has been left out:
> **It was *he* who told me the news.**
> **She is taller than *I*.** (= She is taller than I am.)
>
> Less formal English uses object pronouns, especially when the pronoun stands alone:
> '**Who's there?**' '***Me*, it's *me*, Jimmy.**'
> **I hope that's not *him* again.**
> **She's taller than *me*.**
> **He doesn't know as much as *her*.**

2. Possessive Determiners and Pronouns

2.1 Forms

	Possessive Determiner	*Possessive Pronoun*
Singular		
1st person	**my**	**mine**
2nd person	**your**	**yours**
3rd person		
– masculine	**his**	**his**
– feminine	**her**	**hers**
– general	**one's**	
– with things	**its**	
Plural		
1st person	**our**	**ours**
2nd person	**your**	**yours**
3rd person	**their**	**theirs**

2.2 Possessive determiners

■ Possessive determiners (also called possessive adjectives) are used in the same way as the definite article (⇨ **4.4**). Remember that the choice of determiner depends on the gender of the owner, not of the object owned:

    She's *my* best friend.

■ Nouns referring to groups take either its or their, although its is more usual in American English (⇨ **Nouns, 1.5**):

    The bank doesn't pay *its* staff very well.

■ To emphasize personal ownership, the word own is sometimes added:

    Later that evening he told her the story of his *own* life.
    Does that car belong to the company, or is it your *own*?

▶ Unlike in other languages, possessives can be used before parts of the body:

    I hurt my hand.
    Her head was aching from all the noise.

2.3 Possessive pronouns

■ Possessive pronouns are used in place of 'possessive determiner + noun' when the noun has already been mentioned or is obvious. This is the commonest way of saying that something belongs to somebody (⇨ **Nouns, 3.**):

> 'Whose is this suitcase? Is it *yours* or *mine?*'
> 'I think it's your brother's?'
> You do your work and I'll do *mine*.
> If you haven't got a raincoat, Judy will lend you one of *hers*.

■ It and one do not have possessive pronouns.

3. Reflexive Pronouns

3.1 Forms

	Reflexive Pronoun	Example
Singular	**myself** **yourself** **himself** **herself** **itself**	**I hurt** *myself* **Stop thinking about** *yourself*. **Peter killed** *himself*. **Your mother talks to** *herself*. **This oven turns** *itself* **off.**
Plural	**ourselves** **yourselves** **themselves**	**We felt angry with** *ourselves*. **You should look after** *yourselves*. **They all enjoyed** *themselves*.

3.2 Usage

■ Reflexive pronouns are used:

– if the person or thing that is the subject of the verb is mentioned again later in the same clause, for example as the object or after a preposition. The reflexive pronouns are thus used in the same positions as the object pronouns:

> **He gave** *himself* **the largest portion of chips.**

But note that after prepositions of place the simple object pronoun is used:

> **She saw a man running towards** *her*.
> **Don't look behind** *you*!

– to lay stress on the subject of a sentence:

> *Myself*, **I prefer Chinese food.**
> **Do you know anything about it** *yourself?*

▶ Note that a number of verbs in English require the use of reflexive pronouns:

> **Kevin prides** *himself* **on his work.**
> **We have enjoyed** *ourselves* **very much.**

But this is much rarer than in some languages:

> **I go to bed at eleven p.m. and get up at six thirty. Then I wash and shave.**

3.3 *Each other* v. *one another*

■ If the subject of a verb is two people or groups, and the action of the verb takes place between the two people or groups, the reflexive

pronoun each other is used:
> **We send *each other* cards at Christmas.**
> **They read *each other's* letters with great interest.**

Compare

••

> **Sue and Ted hate themselves.**
> (= Sue hates Sue and Ted hates Ted)
> **Sue and Ted hate each other.**
> (= Sue hates Ted and Ted hates Sue)

••

■ If there are more than two people or groups, **one** another can be used instead of each other:
> **The children are always arguing with *one another*.**

4. The Indefinite and Definite Articles

4.1 The indefinite article: form

■ The indefinite article is a [ə] before a consonant and an [ən] before vowels:

a game ▲ a year ▲ a new boat
an apple ▲ an egg ▲ an old boat

■ However:
– before a word beginning with a vowel which has a consonantal sound e.g. [j, w], a is used:

a university ▲ a union

– before a silent 'h', an is used:

an honour ▲ an hour

4.2 The indefinite article: usage

■ The indefinite article is used only with singular countable nouns (⇨ **Nouns, 2.1**).

■ The indefinite article indicates that the person or thing that follows is a single example but not a particular or identified one:

Valerie's bought *a* new coat.
Can you give me *an* idea of what it will cost?

■ The indefinite article is used in certain other expressions:
– Measurements:

ninety kilometres *an* hour, four times *a* day

– Numerical expressions:

a **couple**
a **dozen**
a **hundred**

– To describe or classify people or things:

My sister's *a* musician.
A whale is *a* mammal.

– In exclamations:

What *a* wonderful view!
What *a* bargain!
BUT **What nice shoes!**

Compare

•••

Be careful not to confuse the article a with the numeral one:

A refrigerator is no good. You need a deep-freeze.
('refrigerator' contrasts with 'deep-freeze')

***One* refrigerator is no good. We've got enough food to fill three.**
('one' contrasts with 'three')

•••

4.3 The definite article: form

The definite article for all types of noun is the:

the book ▴ the boy ▴ the time
the girls ▴ the bicycles ▴ the truth

> The definite article the is pronounced [ðe] before consonant sounds and [ðɪ] before vowel sounds:
> [ðe] **the game ▴ the year ▴ the new boat**
> [ðɪ] **the apple ▴ the eggs ▴ the old boat**
> However, note that:
> – a vowel may have a consonantal sound (e.g. [j, w]); in this case [ðe] is used:
> **the university ▴ the union**
> – before a silent 'h', [ðɪ] is used:
> **the honour ▴ the hour**

4.4 The definite article: usage

■ The can be used before any noun in English.

■ The definite article indicates that the person or thing that follows is a specific example, identifiable from what has been said before:

I saw a policeman. *The* policeman saw me.
***The* bullet hit him in *the* shoulder** (that is, in 'his' shoulder).

■ The is also used when the person or thing is unique or can be identified from our shared knowledge of the world:

***The* sun hasn't shone for a whole week.**
I'm going to *the* station.
Be quiet. I'm on *the* telephone.
I love *the* cinema.
He's in *the* army.
He plays *the* piano.
She went to *the* dentist's.

■ The, used before adjectives, including those for countries, means all the people who the adjective could describe. The verb is plural:

***The* old and *the* poor have suffered greatly.**
Do *the* French take holidays in America?

■ The is also used before the names of newspapers, oceans, seas, rivers, mountain ranges and ships:

The Times ▴ the Atlantic ▴ the Dead Sea ▴ the Thames
the Andes ▴ the Titanic

4.5 Zero article

■ All English nouns have an article except:

– when they have some other determiner (but see **6.11**):

He showed no interest in his job.

– when they are in a list and share the article of the noun or nouns in front of them:

You should wear *a* shirt and tie.
***The* king, queen and princes were executed.**

– when uncountable or plural nouns are used in a 'generic' sense, that is, to indicate the thing or things in general but not any particular example:

I don't like Mondays.
I don't like work.
I don't like French beer.
Life has treated him well.

Compare

I like wine (and drink it often).
I like *the* wine (and want another glass).

■ No article is used before the names of mountains, lakes, streets or roads:

Ben Nevis ▲ Lake Constance ▲ Bond Street ▲ Victoria Station

■ There are furthermore many fixed phrases and types of expression which do not require the use of the article. These can be divided into the following groups:

Place:
be in bed ▲ go to school ▲ go to work ▲ get home ▲ from left to right ▲ in prison ▲ at sea

Time:
in spring ▲ at night ▲ from beginning to end ▲ last night next year

Transport:
come by car ▲ go by bus ▲ arrive on foot

Meals:
have breakfast ▲ invite some friends to dinner

Most titles:
Dr Allen ▲ President Kennedy ▲ King Louis XIV of France

Most countries and continents:
France ▲ England ▲ Europe ▲ South America

BUT **the United States ▲ the British Isles ▲ the Netherlands**
(because these include a countable noun)

Note

He listened to the radio. BUT **He watched television.**
He heard it on the radio. BUT **He saw it on TV.**

5. Numbers, One and Other

Number words are used only before or in place of countable nouns.

determiner	**one book**	**two books**
pronoun	**one**	**two**

5.1 Numbers: forms

Numbers can be either cardinal or ordinal:

■ Cardinal numbers indicate an amount:

0	zero	13	**thirteen**	60	sixty
1	one	14	fourteen	70	seventy
2	two	15	**fifteen**	80	eighty
3	three	16	sixteen	90	ninety
4	four	17	seventeen	100	one hundred
5	five	18	eighteen	110	one hundred and ten
6	six	19	nineteen	200	two hundred
7	seven	20	**twenty**	300	three hundred
8	eight	21	twenty-one	501	five hundred and one
9	nine	22	twenty-two	1000	one thousand
10	ten	30	**thirty**	2000	two thousand
11	**eleven**	40	**forty**	1000000	one million
12	**twelve**	50	**fifty**		

▶ Bold type indicates the forms which differ from the base form, that is we say fifteen, not fiveteen.

■ Ordinal numbers indicate the order :

1st	**first**	11th	eleventh
2nd	**second**	12th	**twelfth**
3rd	**third**	13th	thirteenth
4th	fourth	40th	**fortieth**
5th	**fifth**	50th	**fiftieth**
6th	sixth	61st	sixty-**first**
7th	seventh	72nd	seventy-**second**
8th	**eighth**	83rd	eighty-**third**
9th	**ninth**	95th	ninety-**fifth**
10th	tenth	101st	one hundred and **first**

▶ These are normally formed by adding -th to the cardinal number – exceptions to this rule are indicated in bold type.

	Different types of numbers: pronunciation
0	generally pronounced *nought* [nɔːt] in British English and *zero* ['zɪərəʊ] in American English
	pronounced [əʊ] in British English when part of a list of figures (such as telephone numbers)
	pronounced *nil* [nɪl] in British English and *zero* in American English when referring to a sports result
	pronounced *love* [lʌv] when referring to a tennis result
100	a hundred (general, non-emphatic)
	one hundred (emphatic, *one* hundred rather than *two* hundred)
120	a hundred *and* twenty (British)
	one hundred twenty (American)
5,617	five thousand six hundred *and* seventeen
	Note the use of the comma (,) to indicate thousands
5.617	five *point* six one seven
	Note the use of the full stop (.) to indicate decimal places
3/5	three-fifths
1½	one *and* a half [wʌnənə'hɑːf]
	Note that this is followed by a plural noun and singular or plural verb:
	one and a half metres *isn't/aren't* enough
1906	(date) nineteen oh [əʊ] six
1900	(date) nineteen hundred
472291	(phone number) four seven double two nine one

5.2 Numbers: usage

■ When used as determiners, numbers go after other determiners but before any adjectives:

DET + NUMBER + ADJ + N
my *two* best friends
her *third* husband

■ When used as pronouns, ordinal numbers are usually preceded by the, my, etc:

They accepted one of my ideas but rejected *the other* two.
I've had two meals today already. This is *my/the* third.

■ Hundred, thousand and million have regular plurals when used alone, but have zero plurals when used with other numbers:

Hundreds/thousands/millions of people.
Two hundred/three thousand/six million people.

5.3 *One*

■ One and its plural ones are used to avoid having to repeat countable nouns. They can be preceded by adjectives and determiners:

Which is your car? The black *one* or the red *one*?
This *one* is nicer but that *one* is more expensive.
You can borrow my tools. Which *ones* do you need?

■ The singular one can be used alone, and is thus the singular countable version of some (⇨ **6.1**):

Those cakes look tasty. Can I have *one*, please?

5.4 *Other*

■ Other is used like the number words. It means both 'a new one of the same' and 'a different one'. It is used before nouns as a determiner.

■ When indicating the second of two, other is preceded by the, my, this, etc. When there are more than two possibilities it is usually preceded in the singular by an (written as one word another) and in the plural by some, many, etc:

John was here on Tuesday and *another* friend came to dinner last night. *Some other* friends are coming tonight.
This shoe seems to fit me. Can I try *the other one*?

■ As a pronoun it has the plural form others. (See also **3.3**.):

I bought one book yesterday. Today I bought *another/some others*.
I'll do this job. You can do *the other/the others*.

6. Quantifiers

6.1 Introduction

The chart below shows the commonest quantifiers in English together with the types of nouns which they can precede as determiners and replace as pronouns (⇨ **Nouns, 3.1**):

Determiner/ Pronoun	Countable Singular	Countable Plural	Uncountable
some		some cups	some water
any		any cups	any water
many		many cups	
much			much water
a lot of		a lot of cups	a lot of water
lots of		lots of cups	lots of water
most		most cups	most water
few		few cups	
little			little water
a few		a few cups	
a little			a little water
several		several cups	
no	no cup	no cups	no water
enough		enough cups	enough water
all		all cups	all water
every	every cup		
each	each cup		
either	either cup		
neither	neither cup		
both		both cups	

■ The above quantifiers are looked at in more detail below. Note that most quantifiers can act as both determiners and pronouns, and in most cases below both types of usage are shown. Exceptions to this general rule are indicated.

■ As pronouns, quantifiers are often followed by a phrase beginning with of:

  I like your flowers. Can I take *some (of them)?*
  They haven't read *any of* her books.

■ Many quantifiers also have adverbial uses (⇨ **Adverbs and Adverbials**):

  He's *much* too young.
  He's not old *enough.*
  I didn't see them *either.*

6.2 *Some, any*

Give me *some* peas. Give me *some* sauce.
He has lots of money but he won't lend me *any*.
That pudding looks tasty. Can I have *some*, please?

■ Both some and any mean 'a certain number or quantity of'. Some is used in positive statements; any is used in negative statements.

■ In questions, some is used when the expected answer is 'yes' and any when the expected answer is 'yes' or 'no' (⇨ Syntax 1, 4.1).

Did you see *some* interesting animals?
Did you see *any* interesting animals?

■ Any can be used with countable singular nouns to indicate that the person or thing that follows is not a particular or identified one:

You can buy it at *any* large department store.

6.3 *Many, much, most, a lot of, lots of*

I don't know *many* people here. Do you know *most* of them?
Pat didn't say *much*. Why do you need so *much* cement?
There were too *many* people.
There are *a lot of* ways to do it, but it will take *lots of* time.

■ Much, many and most are both determiners and pronouns.

■ A lot of and lots of are used as determiners; their pronoun forms are a lot and lots. Lots and lots of are more informal than a lot and a lot of:

Some people arrived on time, but *lots* were late.

■ Much and many are used chiefly in questions and negative sentences (⇨ Syntax 1, 3.5 & 4.1) and after too, how, and so.

■ Much, many, a lot of, and lots of all have the comparative forms more, most (⇨ Adverbs and Adverbials, 2.2). These very common forms may be replaced by the following:

plenty of – used in the same way as a lot of:

There's *plenty of* food to go round.

a good deal of, a great deal of – used only before uncountable nouns:

His disappearance was causing *a good deal of* concern.

a large number of – used only with countable nouns:

A large number of birds migrate in winter.
(⇨ **6.11**).

■ The compounds how much and how many appear in questions as both determiners and pronouns. They are used with or instead of the same kinds of nouns as much and many (⇨ Syntax 1, 4.3):

How much is it?
How much sugar do you take in your tea?
How many people were killed in the war?
How many do you think?

6.4 Few, little

It's a poor country with *few* resources and *little* wealth.

■ Few means 'a small number of'; little means 'a small quantity of'. They are used to contrast with a lot of, many etc. Compare a few, a little.

■ The comparative forms are fewer, fewest; less, least (⇨ **ADJECTIVES, 2.3**).

■ Few and little are rare as pronouns.

6.5 A few, a little

To make this cake, I need *a few* raisins and *a little* milk.
I had already met *a few* of the guests.
You'll find with this paint that *a little* goes a long way.

■ A few means 'some but not many'; a little means 'some but not much'. They are both determiners and pronouns. They are used to contrast with no, not any. Compare few, little.

6.6 Several

Several of my friends have been ill recently.
It happens *several* times a day.

■ Several means 'more than a few but less than a lot of'.

6.7 No

I want *no* smoking or drinking in this house.
My personal life is *no* concern of yours.

■ No (= not any) is only a determiner. The corresponding pronoun is none:

None of this is your fault.

6.8 Enough

Have you got *enough* books?
Have you got *enough* time?
He's done some work, but not nearly *enough*.
I've heard *enough* of your lies!

■ Enough means 'a sufficient quantity of'.

6.9 All, every, each

All actors want to win an Oscar.
I didn't understand *all* of what he said.
Every machine in the factory was working properly.

■ When referring to a group of people or things, all is used to mean the whole group. It is used with plural countable nouns or uncountable nouns.

■ **Every** is also used when we are thinking of a whole group, but it stresses that we mean all members of the group without exception. It is used with singular countable nouns and takes a singular verb. Note that **every** is not used as a pronoun.

> **The company gave *every* worker a bonus.**
> ***Every* car has a steering wheel.**

■ **Each** is used to refer to all things in a group when you are thinking of the people or things in the group individually. It is used with singular countable nouns and takes a singular verb:

> **The company gave *each* of its managers a bonus.**
> **The company gave them £20 *each*.**

■ **All** can be used with singular countable nouns for periods of time:

> **It rained *all day*.**
> **I worked *all summer*.**

6.10 *Either, neither, both*

> **You can borrow *either* dictionary, but *neither* is much good.**
> ***Both* your parents were there. *Both* of them had a good time.**

■ **Either** means 'one of two'; neither means 'none of two'. Both means 'two of two'.

■ **Neither of** can be followed by a singular or plural verb:

> ***Neither of them wants/want* to go.**

6.11 Combining determiners and quantifiers

■ Normally a noun is preceded by *either* the article *or* a quantifier:

> **Can I have *the* menu?**
> **Can I have *some* potatoes?**

▶ But note that all, half and both can combine with an article or another determiner:

> ***All the* people at the meeting agreed with me.**
> ***Half a* pencil is better than nothing at all.**

■ **All (of)**, lots of, a lot of, plenty of, and similar expressions can appear before countable singular nouns when followed by another determiner such as the or this:

> ***All (of)* this book is boring.**
> **I saw *a lot of* trees. I saw *a lot of* grass. I saw *a lot of* the country.**

7. Indefinite Pronouns

7.1 Forms

somebody	anybody	everybody	nobody
someone	anyone	everyone	no one
something	anything	everything	nothing

Somebody came running out of the shop.
Has *anyone* phoned today?
Everything is going well and *everyone* seems happy.
I saw *no one* that I knew.

Note the pronunciation of nothing ['nʌθɪŋ].

7.2 Usage

■ The forms ending with -**body** and -**one** refer to people. The forms ending with -**thing** refer to things.

■ The use of the **some**- and **any**- forms is parallel to that of the determiners and pronouns some and any (⇨ **6.2**):
   Someone told me the news about Frank.

■ All the indefinite pronouns, including the **every**- forms, take singular verbs. However, they can take plural personal pronouns and determiners (⇨ **1.1**):
   Nobody here *speaks* Italian.
   Everyone is going to need *their* raincoat(s).

■ The indefinite pronouns are the only pronouns in English which regularly take adjectives. The adjective follows the pronoun.
   Jenny's always saying *something stupid*.
   No one important came to the meeting.
   Is there *anything left*?

■ They also have possessive forms, made in the usual way for nouns (⇨ **Nouns, 3.1**):
   I hope I haven't been wasting *everybody's* time.

For more information on negative forms, see **Syntax 1, 3.2**.

■ Several common adverbs are formed using **some**-, **any**-, etc. However, not all the possible combinations actually exist – consult your dictionary if you are uncertain which combinations are possible.
   He should be arriving *any time* soon.
   I've looked for my glasses *everywhere*.
   I think he'll manage it *somehow*.

8. Demonstratives

8.1 Forms

Singular	*Plural*
this	**these**
that	**those**

> The demonstrative that is always pronounced [ðæt].
> Compare the conjunction and relative pronoun that,
> pronounced [ðət]. (⇨ **10**.)

8.2 Usage

■ The demonstratives are used as both determiners and pronouns:
   Give me *that* shampoo. Give me *that*.

■ This and these are used for things which are felt to be close in space or time. They are associated with here and now.

■ That and those are used for things which are felt to be farther away. They are associated with there and then.
   ***This* food here is to eat now; *that* over there is for the picnic.**
   He was born in 1905. *That's* a long time ago.
   Isn't *that* your father over there?
   ***This* record is excellent. *This* music is excellent.**
   Which skirt should I wear, *this* one or *that* one?
   I don't like *those* trousers. *These* are a bit better.

But in many cases, either this/these or that/those is possible:
   At *this/that* time people thought the sun went round the earth.
   ***These/Those* are very good ideas.**

However, when there is a strong contrast between two possibilities, it is more usual to use this/these and the other/the others (⇨ **5.4**):
   Edberg is serving from *this* end and Becker receiving at *the* other.

■ Only this/these can be used to refer to something that has not yet been mentioned:
   Listen to *this*! I'm going to tell you a story.

■ As pronouns, only those can be used to refer directly to human beings. In such cases, those is usually followed by a defining phrase or clause:
   ***Those* of you who agree, please raise your hands.**

9. Question Words

Questions words are pronouns/determiners which stand for the person or thing referred to in a question (⇨ **Syntax 1, 4.**). They are sometimes referred to as 'WH- words' as most of them start with the letters 'wh'. The question word is generally placed at the beginning of the sentence.

9.1 *Who, which, what*

Who's got £5 to lend me?
We've got orange juice and milk. *Which* would you prefer?
What films are on in town this week?

■ Who is used only as a pronoun for people:
Who told you the news?
Who did you give the letter to?

■ Which and what can be determiners before all types of nouns. As pronouns, which can stand in place of all types of nouns; what cannot refer to people:
Which football team do you support?
Which of my brothers said that?
What food do you like?

■ Which is used when there is a restricted number of possibilities to choose from; what suggests a much larger choice:
What is that?
What songs do you know?
'That's my car.' '*Which* one?' 'The red one.'

■ Who, which, and what can all act as subjects and objects of verbs and as objects of prepositions:
Who broke the window with a stone?
What did the boy break with a stone?
What did the boy break the window with?

■ As subjects, who, which, and what are used with a plural verb when you are asking about more than one person or thing:
Who is he? *Who* are they?
What is your name? *What* are your other names?

■ When the question word is the subject or part of the subject, the word order is as for statements (⇨ **Syntax 1, 1.**):
Who told you about the party?
What guests will be attending?

When the question word is not the subject, the word order is as for questions (⇨ **Syntax 1, 4.3**):
Who do you want to see?
Which books have you read so far?

When the question word would normally follow a preposition, it is moved to the front of the sentence but the preposition remains in its natural position:

> *Who* did you get this money *from*?
> *Which* restaurant are you eating *at* this evening?

Note

In formal English the preposition can go at the beginning, before the question word:

> *In which* department do you work?
> = Which department do you work in?
> *To whom* did you give my letter?
> = Who did you give my letter to?

9.2 *Whom*

In formal English, **who** has the special form **whom** when it is the object of the clause. It is also used as the object of prepositions:

Subject:

> *Who* saw you? *Who* was arguing with you?

Object:

> *Whom* did you see?

Object of preposition:

> a. *Whom* were you arguing with?
> b. *With whom* were you arguing?

In ordinary English the last example would be **Who were you arguing with?** But **whom** must be used in b), where the preposition is placed in front of the question word. Compare **10.4**.

9.3 *Whose*

Whose is the possessive of **who** and **what**. It is used to ask about the 'owner' of something or the person who 'has' it. It can be used as a determiner before, and a pronoun in place of, all kinds of nouns:

> *Whose* story do you believe?
> *Whose* work is the best?
> *Whose* is that coat? *Whose* are those coats?
> *Whose* house did you leave it at?

9.4 *Whichever, whatever, whoever*

Whichever and **whatever** are used in exactly the same ways as **which** and **what**. **Whoever** is used like **who**. They differ from the forms without -ever in showing greater surprise or interest:

> *Whatever* did he say to that?
> *Whoever* do they think they are?

9.5 Other question words

The other question words in English are mostly adverbs. They are usually placed at the beginning of the sentence and the word order is as for other question words (⇨ **Syntax 1, 4.3**):

'*How* do you know?' 'George told me.'
'*When* did you meet her?' 'On Tuesday evening.'
'*Where* are you going?' 'I'm on my way home.'
'*Why* are you angry with me?' 'Because you were rude to my mother.'
'*How much* does it cost?' 'More than you can afford.'

9.6 Indirect questions

All the question words are used in indirect questions (⇨ **Syntax 2, 7.**):

He asked me *who* I was, *where* I lived, and *what* I was doing.
We haven't decided *which* shop we are going to buy it at.

10. Relative Pronouns

> She's the girl *who/that* broke my heart.
> That's the stone *which/that* broke the window.
> Are you the witness *(who/that)* the police are looking for?
> I'm the man *whose* wife has just had a baby.

A relative pronoun introduces a relative clause (⟶ **Syntax 2, 2.**). A relative clause is a clause that tells you something about a noun, rather like an adjective. The relative pronoun takes the place of the noun within the relative clause:

> There is the dog. + The dog bit me.
> → There is the dog *that* bit me.

That is the relative pronoun. That bit me is the relative clause.

10.1 Forms

The main relative pronouns are:

For people:	**who, that**
For things:	**which, that**

The relative pronoun (and conjunction) that is pronounced [ðət]; the demonstrative that is pronounced [ðæt].

10.2 Usage

Relative pronouns can act as subjects or objects. When they are the objects of prepositions, the preposition is usually left at its usual position towards the end of the relative clause. Compare **9.1**.

> That's the stone *(that)* he broke the window *with*.

10.3 Omission

■ The relative pronoun can be omitted, especially in spoken English, when it functions as:

– the object:

> Have you asked everyone *(who/that)* you know?
> Isn't that the dress *(which/that)* you wanted?

– the object of a preposition:

> They're the friends *(who/that)* we had dinner with.
> The tents *(which/that)* we were sleeping in were blown away.

■ However, it cannot be left out:

– if it is the subject of the relative clause:

> The manager *who* hired me has now left the company.
> This is the train *that/which* leaves in ten minutes.

– if it goes with a preposition and the preposition is moved to the beginning of the relative clause. In this case, whom (⇨ **10.4**) is used for people and which for things. That cannot be used.

He is the man *about whom* I warned you.
= He is the man (who/whom/that) I warned you about.

The chair *on which* she was standing suddenly collapsed.
= The chair (which/that) she was standing on suddenly collapsed.

10.4 *Whom*

Whom is used in formal English instead of who where the relative pronoun is not the subject of the relative clause. (⇨ **9.2**, **10.3**):

Have you asked everyone *whom* you know?
They're the friends *whom* we had dinner with.

10.5 *Whose*

Whose is the possessive case of who and sometimes of which. Compare **9.3**.

That is the passenger. + Her bags were stolen.
→ That is the passenger *whose* bags were stolen.

Isn't that the girl *whose* picture was in all the newspapers?

I know the people at *whose* house you stayed.
= I know the people *whose* house you stayed at.

In the garden was a tree *whose* branches hung out over the wall.

10.6 *What*

What is used to mean 'that which, the thing/things which'. In other words, what combines a personal pronoun for a thing with a following relative pronoun:

I don't agree with *what* you said.
What I want is a long, cool drink.

10.7 *Where, when*

Where and when can also be used as relative pronouns. Compare **9.5**.

I couldn't find the house *where* she lived.
That was the day *when* my cat died.

Adjectives

1. Use of Adjectives

1.1 Form

Adjectives in English do not change according to the type of noun they go with.

> an *old* woman ⸱ an *old* man
> *old* women ⸱ *old* men

1.2 Position

■ Most adjectives can appear in three different positions:

– Before nouns. The order of words before nouns is:

> *DET + ADJ + N*
> **green onions**
> **my *dirty old* jeans**
> **these three *expensive new cut-glass* flower vases**

– After linking verbs like be, seem, look, get, become:

> **Your hands are *dirty*.**
> **That doesn't seem *right* to me.**

– At the start of phrases. Adjective phrases usually follow the noun they describe. But, especially when describing a pronoun, they can be placed at the beginning or end of a clause:

> **Burgundy is a region *famous* for its wines.**
> ***Weary* after their long day, the children were soon asleep.**
> **I started to run, by now *certain* that someone was following me.**

■ Some adjectives occur only before nouns. These are called *attributive* adjectives:

> **You are a *complete* idiot.**
> **This is the *main* thing that I wanted to say to you.**

Others, such as ill, well, fond of, occur only after verbs like be and seem or at the start of phrases. These are called *predicative* adjectives. A number of these words begin with a-, including awake, asleep, afraid, ashamed, aware:

> **I'm sorry that Lucy's been *ill*. I'm very *fond* of her.**
> **By now I was wide *awake*.**
> ***Afraid* of what might happen, I decided not to go.**

1.3 Order of adjectives

A *tatty old red, white,* and *blue British* flag flapped in the wind.

When several adjectives are used to describe a single noun, they are placed in the following order:

1. Adjectives that always precede nouns (⇨ **1.2**), e.g. a total disaster, a real pleasure, my only true friend.
2. Adjectives reflecting the speaker's attitude, e.g. a nice day.
3. Adjectives describing size, shape, and other measurable qualities, e.g. a big parcel, the square box, some rich men.
4. Adjectives of age, e.g. a new car, an aged relative.
5. Colour adjectives, e.g. a black dog, a blue line.
6. Adjectives of nationality, e.g. an Italian restaurant.
7. Adjectives describing materials, e.g. a woollen jacket.
8. Adjectives derived from nouns which cannot have comparison, e.g. a moral problem, this industrial dispute.

The following examples are very unlikely but illustrate the method of ordering. Before nouns, the use of commas is partly optional. Elsewhere, the adjectives are separated with commas and the last pair is separated with and (or or):

She has a lovely old blue and white ceramic teapot.

He's the only nice tall, dark and handsome young man that I know.

I'm looking for some genuine old red and green, Indian or Chinese ceremonial costumes.

She was tired, wet, hungry and utterly depressed.

1.4 Adjectives used as nouns

■ Some adjectives can be used after the to form plural nouns referring to groups of people. Note that these adjectives take a plural verb:

The old and needy deserve all our help and assistance.

This film will appeal to *the young at heart.*

■ Adjectives are not used in this way in the singular. A noun must be added:

a blind man
a poor person

1.5 Participles used as adjectives

■ The -ing form and past participle of certain verbs are used as adjectives. Some examples are:

tiring	tired
interesting	interested
boring	bored
exciting	excited

It is important not to confuse the meanings of these pairs of adjectives.

The -**ing** form is active in meaning. It tells us what other people think about the subject of the sentence.

The past participle is passive in meaning. It tells us what the subject of the sentence thinks or feels.

Compare

●●

He is *boring*. (= other people think he is boring)
He is *bored*. (= he thinks someone or something is boring)

●●

2. Comparison of Adjectives

2.1 Forms

Absolute	a tall tree	an honest man
Comparative	a taller tree	a more honest man
Superlative	the tallest tree in the garden	the most honest man in the company

2.2 Regular comparison

■ English uses two ways of forming comparative and superlative forms of adjectives:

1. By adding -er for the comparative and -est for the superlative. This class includes:

– all one-syllable adjectives:

> **fast** < **faster** < **fastest**
> **strong** < **stronger** < **strongest**

– some two-syllable adjectives (mainly those ending in -y, -le and -ow):

> **quiet** < **quieter** < **quietest**
> **dirty** < **dirtier** < **dirtiest**
> **simple** < **simpler** < **simplest**
> **narrow** < **narrower** < **narrowest**

– three-syllable adjectives consisting of un- plus a two-syllable adjective which adds -er and -est:

> **unhappy** < **unhappier** < **unhappiest**

Note spelling changes:

a. A single consonant is doubled after a short vowel:

> **big** < **bigger** < **biggest** ▲ **fat** < **fatter** < **fattest**

b. Final -y changes to -i- before -er and -est:

> **silly** < **sillier** < **silliest** ▲ **unhappy** < **unhappier** < **unhappiest**

c. Adjectives ending in -e add simply -r and -st:

> **little** < **littler** < **littlest** ▲ **rude** < **ruder** < **rudest**

2. By use of the words **more** (for the comparative) and **most** (for the superlative). This class includes:

– all three-syllable adjectives (except those mentioned above):

> **beautiful** < **more beautiful** < **most beautiful**

– the majority of two-syllable adjectives (including all those which end in -ful, -less, -al, -ant, -ent, -ic, -ive, -ous, or begin with a-):

> **distant** < **more distant** < **most distant**
> **graceful** < **more graceful** < **most graceful**

– all participles:

boring < more boring < most boring
spoilt < more spoilt < most spoilt

(Though a few very common ones can also use -er and -est, e.g. tired)

■ Note that many two-syllable adjectives can form their comparisons in both ways:

common	<	commoner/	<	commonest/
		more common		most common
clever	<	cleverer/	<	cleverest/
		more clever		most clever

Others have only one possibility and need to be learned separately.

■ When in doubt, use more and most. It rarely sounds badly wrong, especially in British English, while using -er and -est where they do not belong can sound very unnatural.

2.3 Irregular comparison

The following adjectives and determiners have irregular comparison:

Absolute	*Comparative*	*Superlative*
good	better	best
bad	worse	worst
much/many	more	most
little	less	least
few	fewer/less	fewest/least
far	farther/further	farthest/furthest

Note

In British English, farther and further are both used to talk about distance. In American English, only farther is used.

2.4 Comparison of adjectives: use

Comparative

■ The comparative is used when two things are compared:

London is *bigger* than Paris.

■ Than is used to indicate direct comparison. Than can be followed by a clause or by a noun or pronoun:

The exam was *easier than I expected.*
Gregory appeared to be *more confused than his sister.*
Carol gave you *a nicer present than (she gave) me.*
My dad's *bigger than yours.*

▬ Note ▬

When **than** is followed by a personal pronoun, the object pronoun is used in everyday English. In formal English, however, the subject pronoun is used:

Informal: **He's bigger than me.**
Formal: **He's bigger than I (am).**

Informal: **Keith has a faster car than me.**
Formal: **Keith has a faster car than I (do).**

■ Difference can be emphasized with much, far or a lot and limited with a little (bit) or rather:
He's *much* older than his wife.
Are you feeling *a little (bit)* better today?

■ To show that something is gradually increasing or decreasing, English uses two comparatives separated by and:
It's getting *colder and colder*.
He became *more and more* anxious with every passing minute.

■ The comparative is used with the to show that a relationship exists between two developments or actions:
The *more* he thought about it, the *worse* the situation seemed.
The *older* she got, the *more* bitter she became.

When using this construction, take care with word order. More usually goes with the adjective, adverb or noun:
The *more* interesting it is, the *more* attention they pay.
NOT **The more it is interesting…**

Superlative

■ The superlative is used when selecting from a group of more than two. It is usually preceded by the or some equivalent determiner such as my.
Henry's *the worst* child in the whole school.
It was *the happiest* day of my life.
We all went down to *our nearest* pub.
Jane's *best* subject is physics.

■ Both comparatives and superlatives are often used after the without a noun directly following:
This is *the likelier* of the two possibilities.
All the babies were noisy, but Betty's was *the noisiest*.

Other types of Comparison

■ To compare 'downwards', English uses less and least before adjectives of all kinds:
The film was *less enjoyable* than I'd hoped.
As time went on, he became *less and less happy* about his job.
This is the *least interesting* part of the book.

■ A similar meaning can be shown by using **so...as** and **as...as** in negative sentences. The difference is shown by these examples:

A mouse is not *as big as* **a rat** (though neither of them is big).

An elephant is not *so big as* **a whale** (but both of them are big).

■ In positive sentences as... as... is used to show equality:

My uncle is *as strong as* **an ox.**

I'll do it *as soon as* **I can.**

The Noun Phrase

1.1 Introduction

A noun phrase is a phrase whose most important word is a noun (the 'head' noun). Noun phrases have several uses (in the following examples, the whole noun phrase is in bold and the 'head' noun in bold italic print):

As Subject of a Verb:

> **The little *dog*** was sleeping in its basket.

As Object of a Verb:

> I enjoyed **the *story* about your sister**.

As Complement of a Verb:

> This is **the best *film*** that I've ever seen.

After a Preposition:

> He works in **a *school* for deaf children**.

As Adverbial:

> I phone my parents **every *week***.

1.2 Order of elements in the noun phrase

As is clear from the above examples, a noun phrase can have other elements both before and after the 'head' noun. The order of these elements is more or less fixed.

Elements before the 'head' noun

1. Determiners & Possessives	*2.* Adjectives	*3.* Nouns	*Head Noun*
an	exciting	murder	mystery
both my	black and white	cotton	shirts
any	up-to-date	train	timetables
Sandy's two	nice, new	pure-wool	sweaters

1. Determiners and -'s Possessives

■ The determiners and -'s possessive nouns always come first in the noun phrase (⇨ **PRONOUNS AND DETERMINERS, 6.11**). If there is more than one item, the order is as follows:

  a. all, both, half; double, twice, etc:
> **all this food, both my friends;**
> **double this amount, once a day**

  b. other determiners and -'s possessives, e.g.:
> **a, the, some, those, Jean's, my parents', etc.**

  c. numbers and other quantifiers, e.g. much, many:
> **the first three runners, Bill's many admirers**

The Noun Phrase

■ Note that **Bill's many admirers** means 'all Bill's admirers, and there are many of them'. To express the meaning 'many people from the group of Bill's admirers', the quantifier is moved to the front and followed by of:

many of Bill's admirers
a third of the work ⸌ most of this money

2. Adjectives

■ Verb participles can act like adjectives and therefore come into the same category, e.g. falling prices, broken glass. (⇨ **ADJECTIVES, 1.1**)

■ Some short phrases, especially prepositional phrases, can also act as adjectives. Such phrases are often joined by hyphens to help the reader see which words go together.

a very *down-to-earth* attitude

■ Note that the adjectives can also be modified, e.g. a highly unlikely story. For the order of adjectives, see **ADJECTIVES, 1.3**.

3. Nouns

■ English uses modifying nouns before 'head' nouns very freely (⇨ **NOUNS, 4.**):

a Christmas card ⸌ a plastic bucket
our Paris design department

Elements following the 'head' noun

	Head noun	Element	Type of element
	President	elect	*1. Adjective*
a	**piece**	of cake	*2. Prepositional*
the	**house**	on the corner	*phrase*
the	**reason**	why we came	*3. Defining clause*
the	**cat**	asleep on the chair	*4. Adjective phrase*
all	**people**	wanting to buy tickets	*5. -ing clause*
a	**school**	known for its sportsmen	*6. Past participle clause*
your	**chance**	to make things better	*7. 'to' infinitive clause*
the	**woman**	who teaches us Spanish	*8. Relative clause*

1. Such adjectives are rare. Note that adjectives always follow pronoun 'heads' (⇨ **PRONOUNS AND DETERMINERS, 7.2**),

something strange ⸌ no one interesting.

2. See **SYNTAX 1,1; ADVERBS AND ADVERBIALS.**

3. See **PRONOUNS AND DETERMINERS, 10.**
4. See **ADJECTIVES, 1.**
5. See **VERBS 3, 5.**
6. See **VERBS 3, 6.**
7. See **VERBS 3, 4.**
8. See **SYNTAX 2, 2.**

■ The order of these elements is not always fixed and there can be some variation:

I'm having a *party* on Saturday for all my friends.
= I'm having a *party* for all my friends on Saturday.

But the following general tendencies usually apply:

– Single adjectives always follow directly after the 'head' noun.

– Shorter elements usually precede longer elements; for instance, prepositional phrases usually come before relative clauses:

The *girl* in our class who comes from Scotland.
rather than
The *girl* who comes from Scotland in our class.

– Items which define the 'head noun' usually precede items which merely describe it:

The *collection* of modern art at the Tate Gallery.
The *man* I told you about, who works with my brother.

– Items containing stressed elements usually come after items without special stress. For instance, if someone is looking for a particular book in a room where there are books everywhere, you might say:

It's the *book* with the blue cover on the shelf.

but if all the books in the room are on the shelf, you would be more likely to say:

It's the *book* on the shelf with the blue cover.

Verbs 1

1. Main Verbs – Forms
take, takes, taking; took; taken

2. Auxiliary Verbs
be, have, do

3. Modal Auxiliaries
can/could ⸱ may/might ⸱ will/would
shall/should ⸱ must ⸱ ought to/need/dare

4. Phrasal and Prepositional Verbs
take up ⸱ take to

5. The Complementation of Verbs
try to take ⸱ enjoy taking

1. Main Verbs – Forms

Except for be (⇨ **2.1**), no English verb has more than five different forms. Taking the example of the verb write, they are:

– the base form: write.

– the -s form (or third person singular): She *writes* letters.

– the -ing form (or present participle): I *was writing* a letter.

– the past tense form: I *wrote* a letter.

– the past participle: I *have written* a letter.

1.1 The base form

The base form is used:

a. In the simple present tense:
   I *write* letters. (⇨ **Verbs 2, 1.1**)

b. After the modals and do, and after make and let (but see **5.2**)
   I don't *understand*.
   I shall *write* a letter. (⇨ **3.6**)
   Let's *go*.
   She made him *tell* her everything.

c. For the imperative:
   ***Write* me a letter.** (⇨ **Verbs 3, 1.**)

d. For the present subjunctive:
   I insisted that he *write* a letter. (⇨ **Verbs 3, 2.**)

e. After *to* in the *to* infinitive:
  I want *to write* a letter. (⟹ **VERBS 3, 4.**)

1.2 The *-s* form

■ The -s form is used only for the third person singular of the simple present tense (⟹ **VERBS 2, 1.1**):
  She *writes* letters.

■ The -s form is made by adding -s to the base form:
take–takes	open–opens
see–sees	read–reads

Note the following variations in spelling. When the base form ends:
– -o, -ss, -sh, -ch, -x, -z, the -s form is base form + -es, e.g. fixes, washes.
– consonant + -y, the -y of the base form becomes -ies: tries, replies.
– vowel + -y, the ending is base form + -s: enjoys, plays.

a. Verbs ending in the sound [f, k, p, t, θ] add the sound [-s]:
she laughs/makes/drops/sits/baths
b. Verbs ending in [b, d, ð, g, l, m, n, ŋ, v] and all vowels add the sound [-z]:
she robs/needs/breathes/nags/kills/comes/wins/sings/loves; enters/plays/lies/sees/flows
c. Nouns ending in [dʒ, s, ʃ, tʃ, z, ʒ] add the sound [-ɪz]:
she damages/misses/fixes/wishes/snatches/amazes
Compare the rules for the -s plural (⟹ **NOUNS,1.1**) and the -'s possessive (⟹ **NOUNS, 3.1**) of nouns.

Irregular forms

The only important exceptions to these rules are:

be	→	**is** [ɪz]	
have [hæv]	→	**has** [hæz]	(⟹ **2.1**)
do [duː]	→	**does** [dʌz]	
say [seɪ]	→	**says** [sez]	
go [gəʊ]	→	**goes** [gəʊz]	

1.3 The *-ing* form

The -ing form is used:
a. In progressive tenses:
  I was *writing* a letter. (⟹ **VERBS 2, 1.4 & 2.4**)
b. After certain verbs:
  I enjoy *writing* letters. (⟹ **VERBS 1, 5.1**)
c. In reduced relative clauses as a modifier of the head noun:

The man *leaning* against the wall. (⇨ VERBS **3, 5.2**)

d. As a verbal noun:
   Writing letters is fun. (⇨ VERBS **3, 5.2**)

e. As an adjective:
   The talk was *interesting*. (⇨ ADJECTIVES, **1.5**)

■ The -ing form is generally made by adding -ing to the base form:
   being, doing, pushing, wanting, reading, saying, trying, carrying

■ But when the base form ends in:

– consonant + -e, the -e is dropped before -ing:
   have → having ⸳ like → liking ⸳ come → coming
   translate → translating ⸳ handle → handling

If the consonant is a g, the -e is kept:
   singe → singeing ⸳ cringe → cringeing

– the letters -ie, the ending becomes -ying:
   die → dying ⸳ lie → lying ⸳ tie → tying

– other vowel combinations, the ending is regular:
   being, seeing, agreeing, skiing

■ When the base form ends in a stressed vowel spelt as one letter + a single consonant, the consonant is doubled:
   rob → robbing ⸳ sit → sitting ⸳ occur → occurring
   admit → admitting

There is no doubling when the vowel is spelt with two letters:
   needing, dreading

Nor when the final syllable is unstressed:
   entering, widening, crediting

Except in the following cases:
   -c → -cking (**panic → panicking**)
   -m → -mming (**program → programming**)
   -p → -pping (**worship → worshipping**)
   -l → -lling (**tunnel → tunnelling**)

Note

In American English, the 'l' is only doubled if the final syllable is stressed:
   travel → traveling → traveled
   rebel → rebelling → rebelled

When the base form ends in:

a. silent -r, the -r is sounded before -ing:

pour [pɔ:] → **pouring** ['pɔ:rɪŋ]
fear [fɪə] → **fearing** ['fɪərɪŋ]

b. unstressed -le, -el, -re, -er or -en, the unstressed vowel [ə] is usually dropped before -ing:

enter ['entə] → **entering** ['entrɪŋ]
travel ['trævəl] → **travelling** ['trævlɪŋ]
fasten ['fɑ:sən] → **fastening** ['fɑ:snɪŋ]

1.4 The past tense form

The past tense form is used:

a. For the simple past tense:

I *wrote* a letter (⇨ **VERBS 2, 2.1**)

b. In certain if clauses:

If I *wrote* a letter, would you answer? (⇨ **SYNTAX 2, 4.**)

c. In reported speech:

He said that he *wrote* lots of letters. (⇨ **SYNTAX 2, 7.2**)

1.5 The past participle

The past participle is used:

a. In perfect tenses:

I have *written* a letter (⇨ **VERBS 2, 2.6**)

b. In the passive:

The letter was *written* by me (⇨ **VERBS 3, 3.**)

c. As an adjective:

written documents (⇨ **ADJECTIVES, 1.5**)

d. In past participial clauses:

a letter *written* by a friend

1.6 The past tense and the past participle: regular and irregular verbs

	base form	past	past part.
Regular:	ask	asked	asked
	need	needed	needed
Semi-reg.:	feed	fed	fed
	buy	bought	bought
Irregular:	see	saw	seen
	come	came	come

Regular Verbs

■ The past and past participle forms of regular verbs are always the same and can be predicted from the base form:

base form + -ed, e.g.
looked, cheated, failed, seemed, appeared, repaired

■ Note the following changes in spelling:

a. When the base form ends in:

– -e, only -d is added:
hoped, liked, died, judged, debated, invited, agreed

– a consonant + -y, the -y ending becomes -ied:
tried, replied

– a vowel + -y, the ending is regular:
enjoyed, played

Note the spellings of **paid** (pay) and **laid** (lay).

b. When the base form ends in a stressed vowel spelt as one letter + a single consonant, the consonant is doubled. The conditions (and differences between American English and British English) are the same as those for adding -ing (⇨ **1.3**):

flopped, banned, knitted, admitted, barred, referred, panicked, programmed, worshipped, travelled

But note **entered, widened; needed, dreaded**.

> In careful speech, the ending -(e)d is pronounced:
>
> – [-t] if the base form ends in [f, k, p, s, ʃ, tʃ, θ]:
>
> **laughed, picked, hoped, missed, wished, watched**
>
> – [-d] if the base form ends in [b, ð, dʒ, g, l, m, n, ŋ, v, z, ʒ] or a vowel:
>
> **robbed, breathed, damaged, nagged, killed, combed, phoned, banged, loved, surprised; entered, played, sighed, agreed, flowed**
>
> – [-ɪd] if the base form ends in [d] or [t]:
>
> **needed, nodded, eroded; rested, chatted, hated**

Semi-regular verbs

The past and past participle forms of semi-regular verbs are always the same and end in a [-d] or [-t] sound. But this form cannot be predicted from the base. There is often a change in the vowel sound.

Among the commonest semi-regular verbs are:

bend (bent)	**bind (bound)**
bleed (bled)	**breed (bred)**
bring (brought)	**build (built)**
burn[1] (burnt)	**buy (bought)**

catch (caught)
deal (dealt)
dwell[1] (dwelt)
feel (felt)
find (found)
grind (ground)
hear (heard)
keep (kept)
lead (led)
leap[1] (leapt)
leave (left)
light[1] (lit)
make (made)
meet (met)
say (said)
sell (sold)
shoot (shot)
sleep (slept)
smell[1] (smelt)
spell[1] (spelt)
spill[1] (spilt)
spoil[1] (spoilt)
sweep (swept)
tell (told)
understand (understood)
wind (wound)

creep (crept)
dream[1] (dreamt)
feed (fed)
fight (fought)
flee (fled)
have (had)
hold (held)
kneel[1] (knelt)
lean[1] (leant)
learn[1] (learnt)
lend (lent)
lose (lost)
mean (meant)
read (read)
seek (sought)
send (sent)
sit (sat)
slide (slid)
speed[1] (sped)
spend (spent)
spit (spat)
stand (stood)
teach (taught)
think (thought)
weep (wept)

Note

The verbs followed by [1] in the above list can also be regular, especially in American English, e.g. burned, spoiled.

■ The following short verbs, all ending in -d or -t, have the same forms in the base, past and past participle:

bet, burst, cast, cost, cut, hit, hurt, let, put, quit, rid, set, shed, shut, split, spread

How much did it *cost*?
It *cost* eighty pounds.
It should have *cost* more.

The verb **read** has the same forms but different pronunciations:

base form [ri:d]
past and past participle [red].

Irregular Verbs

Irregular verbs can differ in all three forms. The forms cannot be predicted from the base form and do not have to end in [-d] or [-t].

There is some variation in Standard English, e.g.

My pullover shrank/shrunk in the wash.

■ The chart below gives the forms of some common verbs.

Base	Past	Past Part.	Base	Past	Past Part.
be	was	been	bear	bore	borne
beat	beat	beaten	become	became	become
begin	began	begun	bite	bit	bitten
blow	blew	blown	break	broke	broken
choose	chose	chosen	cling	clung	clung
come	came	come	dig	dug	dug
do	did	done	draw	drew	drawn
drink	drank	drunk	drive	drove	driven
eat	ate[1]	eaten	fall	fell	fallen
fling	flung	flung	fly	flew	flown
forbid	forbade	forbidden	foresee	foresaw	foreseen
forget	forgot	forgotten	forgive	forgave	forgiven
freeze	froze	frozen	get	got	got[2]
give	gave	given	go	went	gone/been
grow	grew	grown	hang[3]	hung	hung
hide	hid	hidden	know	knew	known
lie	lay	lain	mistake	mistook	mistaken
mow[3]	mowed	mown	ride	rode	ridden
ring	rang	rung	rise	rose	risen
run	ran	run	see	saw	seen
shake	shook	shaken	shine[3]	shone	shone
show[3]	showed	shown	shrink	shrank/shrunk	shrunk
sing	sang	sung	sink	sank	sunk
sling	slung	slung	speak	spoke	spoken
spin	span/spun	spun	spring	sprang	sprung
steal	stole	stolen	stick	stuck	stuck
sting	stung	stung	stink	stank/stunk	stunk
stride	strode	stridden	strike	struck	struck
swear	swore	sworn	swell[3]	swelled	swollen
swim	swam	swum	swing	swung	swung
take	took	taken	tear	tore	torn
throw	threw	thrown	tread	trod	trodden
wake[3]	woke	woken	wear	wore	worn
weave	wove	woven	win	won	won
write	wrote	written			

⌐ Note

1 ate is usually pronounced [et] in British English and [eɪt] in American English.

2 In American English, the past participle of certain senses of **get** is gotten.

3 These verbs can also be regular, especially in certain senses, e.g.
   He hung the picture. (= put it on the wall)
   He hanged himself. (= killed himself)

2. Auxiliary Verbs

2.1 The verb phrase and auxiliaries

■ In English, ideas like tense, the passive, negation, questions and modality (obligation, possibility, advisability, etc) cannot be expressed by one word as in some other languages. As many as six words may be required:

> **I might not have been being followed.**

All of these words together are called the Verb Phrase. Those words which carry the meaning of the verb phrase are called 'main' verbs. These may occur without auxiliaries in the simple present (⟿ **Verbs 2, 1.1**) and simple past tenses (⟿ **Verbs 2, 2.1**).

> **I** *watch* **the television.**
> **I** *watched* **the television.**

More complex verb phrases, however, include other words called *auxiliaries*, which can themselves be divided into *main auxiliaries* and *modal auxiliaries* (⟿ **3.**). The main auxiliaries are **be, have** and **do,** and the modal auxiliaries are **can, must, should,** etc. Auxiliaries are placed before the main verb and are used for various purposes:

1. To form compound tenses (be and have) (⟿ **Verbs 2**)
   > **I** *have been* **watching the television.**
   > **She** *wasn't* **watching the television.**

2. To form the passive (be) (⟿ **Verbs 3, 3.**)
   > **The television** *is* **watched by everybody.**

3. To form negative sentences and questions (do) (⟿ **Syntax 1, 3.**)
   > *Do* **you watch the television?**
   > **She** *did***n't watch the television.**

4. To form modal sentences (modal auxiliaries) (⟿ **3.**)
   > **I** *must* **watch the television.**

▶ Note that the main auxiliaries **be, have** and **do** have their own meanings as main verbs and can appear on their own as such (see below).

2.2 *Be* as an auxiliary

Present tense

I am	**we are**
you are	**you are**
he/she/it is	**they are**

Past tense

I was	**we were**
you were	**you were**
he/she/it was	**they were**

-ing form: **being**   Past participle: **been**

■ In spoken English you usually use contractions (⇨ **2.6**) in the present tense and before not (⇨ **SYNTAX 1, 3.1**).

■ Even as a main verb, be acts like an auxiliary (⇨ **2.6**):
  'Were you there?' 'No, I wasn't. But Emma was.'

■ The main uses of be as an auxiliary are:

– to form continuous tenses: be + -ing form:
  She is leaving this evening.

– to form the passive: be + past participle:
  Alan was left on his own.

2.3 *Have* as an auxiliary

Present tense
I have	**we have**
you have	**you have**
he/she/it has	**they have**

Past tense and past participle: **had**
-ing form: **having**

■ The main use of have as an auxiliary is to form perfect tenses: have + past participle:
  She had left by the time he got home.

─ **Note** ─

Until recently **have** could also act like an auxiliary when it was the main verb of a clause. Modern American usage treats main verb **have** like any other main verb; in modern British English it is often replaced by have got.

Old-fashioned:
  I haven't any money. Have you any money?
American:
  I don't have any money. Do you have any money?
British:
  I haven't got any money. Have you got any money?

2.4 The verb *do*

Present tense
I do	**we do**
you do	**you do**
he/she/it does	**they do**

Past tense: **did**
Past participle: **done**
-ing form: **doing**

■ The main use of **do** as an auxiliary is to form negative statements and questions when the principal verb is in the simple present or past tense (other tenses use the auxiliaries be or have):

> **Do you know what I mean?**
> **She doesn't need any help.**

■ It is also used for emphasis:

> **You're wrong. I do know her; very well in fact.**

2.5 Verb groups with auxiliaries: the order of auxiliaries

■ When there are two or more auxiliaries before a main verb, their order is fixed. The maximum number of auxiliaries is four, though it is rare to find more than two at a time:

> **I suspected that I...**
> **might   have   been   being   followed.**
> *modal + perfect 'have' + progressive 'be' + passive 'be' + main verb*

■ The form of each part is determined by what precedes it:

– The modals (⇨ **3.**) and the auxiliary do (⇨ **2.4**) are followed by the base form:

  + Main verb: **I *can* see you.**
                    We *did*n't say anything.
  + Perfect have: **She *should have* known better.**
  + Progressive be: **I *will be* working tonight.**
  + Passive be: **He *must be* caught immediately.**

– Perfect have (⇨ **2.3**) is followed by the past participle:

  + Main verb: **I *have* never liked you.**
  + Progressive be: **Have *you been* drinking?**
  + Passive be: **The money *has been* stolen.**

– Progressive be (⇨ **Verbs 2, 1.4**) is followed by the -ing form:

  + Main verb: **Why *are you staring* at me?**
  + Passive be: **My suit *is being* mended.**

– Passive be (⇨ **Verbs 3, 3.**) is followed by the past participle:

  + Main verb: **The work *was done* badly.**

2.6 Auxiliary verbs: special properties

All verbs acting as auxiliaries, along with be when it is a main verb, have the following unique properties:

■ They have contracted forms, especially before not (⇨ **2.7**):

> **He's gone away. She *won't* come.**
> **They *don't* know. I'm sorry.**

■ They appear before the subject in questions (⇨ **2.8**):

> **Can I come?**
> **Do you speak English?**
> **Were you there?**

■ They can appear alone with the subject to avoid repetition of the main verb (⇨ **2.8; Syntax 1, 4.5**):

> I worked much harder than *you did*.
> 'Would you like some tea?' 'Yes, *I would*.'/'No, *I wouldn't*.'

■ When stressed, it is not the meaning of the auxiliary that is emphasized but that of the whole sentence:

> Don't be angry with him. He HAS paid me now.
> I can't speak German but I CAN speak French.
> Oh, but you're wrong; I DO care.
> You may not believe me, but she IS my mother.

2.7 Contracted forms of auxiliaries

In normal spoken English, and in informal written English, verbs used as auxiliaries (and main verb *be*) often appear in contracted forms. Only *be*, *have*, *will/shall* and *would/should* have contracted forms in positive sentences. All the auxiliaries except **may** have contracted forms incorporating the word **not**.

Contracted forms are particularly common in negative questions:

> Can't you find it? *rather than* Can you not find it?
> Doesn't he agree? *rather than* Does he not agree?

Positive Contractions

Be. Only the present tense forms have contractions:

I'm going [aɪm]	we're going [wɪə]
you're going [juə]	you're going [juə]
he's/she's/it's going	they're going [ðɛə]
[hiːz/ʃiːz/ɪts]	

■ The -'s contraction for *is* can be added to (the last word of) the subject of any sentence.

> *It's* all right.
> *My dog's* dead.
> *That man over there's* my boss.

> The -'s contraction follows the same pronunciation rules as the -'s possessive (⇨ **Nouns, 3.1**).

■ In writing, -'re is usually added only to subject personal pronouns:

> You're right.
> They're wrong.

Have. Both the present and past tense forms have contractions:

have → -'ve:	*They've* got a flat in Paris.	
	I've been robbed.	
has → -'s:	*She's* gone away.	
	Hilary's met the Queen.	
had → -'d:	*I'd* decided to go.	
	You'd better be quiet.	

■ The -'s contraction for **has** can be added to (the last word of) the subject of any sentence.

> The -'s contraction for **has** follows the same pronunciation rules as for -'s possessive (⇨ **NOUNS, 3.1**).
>
> -'ve and -'d are pronounced [-v] and [-d].

■ In writing, the contractions -'ve and -'d are usually added only to subject pronouns.

Will/shall. Will and shall, and **would** and **should**, become identical when joined to preceding words.

> will/shall → -'ll:
> *I'll* come tomorrow.
> *It'll* be all right.
> would/should → -'d:
> He said *he'd* help me.
> *I'd* rather have tea.

> -'ll and -'d are pronounced [-l] and [-d], except in it'll ['ɪtəl] and it'd ['ɪtəd].

■ In writing, the contractions -'ll and -'d are usually added only to subject pronouns.

Compare

••

The -'s contraction can stand for both **is** and **has**.

> **She's forgotten.**
> = a. **She is forgotten.** (people do not remember her)
> = b. **She has forgotten.** (she does not remember)

Remember that -'s for **has** appears only in perfect tense sentences and is always followed by a past participle.

The -'d contraction can stand for both **had** and **would/should**:

> **I wish that he'd come.**
> = a. **I wish that he had come.**
> = b. **I wish that he would come.**

Remember that -'d for **had** appears only in past perfect sentences and is always followed by a past participle; -'d for **would/should** is always followed by a base form.

••

Negative contractions

Be

>are [ɑ:, ə] → **aren't** ['ɑ:nt]:
>*Aren't* you Frank's sister?
>
>is [ɪz] → **isn't** ['ɪzənt]:
>I hope it *isn't* too cold.
>
>was [wɒz, wəz] → **wasn't** ['wɒzənt]:
>She *wasn't* very pleased.
>
>were [wɜ:] → **weren't** ['wɜ:nt]:
>Why *weren't* you at work?

■ Am not has no contracted form in ordinary statements. The positive contraction + not is used instead:

>*I'm not* sure what to do.

■ In negative questions, etc am not contracts to aren't:

>*Aren't I* going to see you again?
>I am right, *aren't I?*

Have

>have [hæv, əv] → **haven't** ['(h)ævənt]:
>We *haven't* eaten yet.
>
>has [hæz, əz] → **hasn't** ['(h)æzənt]:
>He *hasn't* got it.
>
>had [hæd, əd] → **hadn't** ['(h)ædənt]:
>I wish we *hadn't* come.

Do

>do [du:, də] → **don't** [dəʊnt]:
>I *don't* live here.
>
>does [dʌz, dəz] → **doesn't** ['dʌzənt]:
>She *doesn't* agree.
>
>did [dɪd] → **didn't** ['dɪdənt]:
>Why *didn't* you tell me?

The modals

>can [kæn, kən] → **can't** [kɑ:nt]:
>Sally *can't* dance.
>
>could [kʊd, kəd] → **couldn't** ['kʊdənt]:
>I *couldn't* help it.
>
>will [wɪl] → **won't** [wəʊnt]:
>He *won't* help me.
>
>would [wʊd, wəd] → **wouldn't** ['wʊdənt]:
>Why *wouldn't* she tell me?
>
>shall [ʃæl, ʃəl] → **shan't** [ʃɑ:nt]:
>I *shan't* answer you!
>
>should [ʃʊd, ʃəd] → **shouldn't** ['ʃʊdənt]:
>You *shouldn't* fight.

might [maɪt] → **mightn't** ['maɪtənt] :
He *mightn't* have come.

must [mʌst] → **mustn't** [kæn, kən]:
You *mustn't* be so noisy.

need [niːd] → **needn't** ['niːdənt]:
You *needn't* pay me now.

dare [dɛə] → **daren't** [dɛənt]:
I *daren't* think about it.

▶ Note that the uncontracted form of can is written as one word cannot. May [meɪ] and used to ['juːstʊ] usually have no contracted forms. Ought not to [ɔːt'nɒttə] appears occasionally as oughtn't to ['ɔːtəntə].

2.8 Auxiliaries and word order

Subject-auxiliary inversion

■ In normal English word order, the subject comes before the verb (⇨ **SYNTAX 1, 1.**):

SUBJECT + AUXILIARY + VERB + ...
Brian can borrow your records.
You have been seeing him again.

This is true of negative statements too:

SUBJECT + FIRST AUXILIARY + not + VERB + ...
I won't see you tomorrow.

■ However, in most questions the first auxiliary appears before the subject (⇨ **SYNTAX 1, 4.**):

(WH- WORD +) AUXILIARY + SUBJECT + VERB + ...
Can Brian borrow your records?
Have you been seeing him again?

Even with tenses which do not require auxiliary verbs (simple present and past tense), the auxiliary do must be used in questions and negatives. In questions it will appear before the verb (⇨ **SYNTAX 1, 4.**):

I have to work today.
→ *Do I* have to work today?
→ *I don't* have to work today.

Susan likes bright clothes.
→ *Does Susan* like bright clothes?
→ *Susan doesn't* like bright clothes.

They met last week.
→ *When did they* meet?
→ *They didn't* meet here.

Subject + auxiliary in shortened sentences

■ The subject and first auxiliary (or main verb be) are often used alone when the main verb has been used already and therefore does not need to be repeated. If necessary, the appropriate form of do is supplied (⇨ **2.4**). The information that followed the main verb can also be omitted:

I worked late but *he didn't.* (= ...but he didn't work late.)
Sandra wants to go to Greece again but *I don't.*
(= ...but I don't want to go to Greece again.)

■ This omission of the main verb is particularly common in questions and answers to questions (⇨ **SYNTAX 1, 4.**):
'I speak Russian. *Do you?*'
'I like coffee. *Do you?*'

Yes or no is usually sufficient to answer such a question, but a shortened sentence consisting of the subject plus the first auxiliary is often added. Negative questions in particular demand a fuller reply:
'I like coffee. Do you?' 'Yes(, I do).'/'No(, I don't).'
'Doesn't Tom work with you?' 'Yes, he does.'/ 'No, he doesn't.'
'Could the cat have eaten it?' 'I suppose it could.'

Other types of questions are often answered in the same way:
'Who sold you that car?' 'Margaret did.'

■ The subject and auxiliary are also used together in:
– other shortened comments:
'I don't like meat.' *'Neither do I.* But *Debbie does.'*
'I'll hit you.' 'No, *you won't. You can't.* You're too small.'
I'd like to come but I'm afraid *I can't.*

– tag questions and their responses (⇨ **SYNTAX 1, 4.5**):
'I am right, *aren't I?*' 'Yes, *you are.*'/'No, *you aren't.*'
'He won't break it, *will he?*' 'Yes, *he will.*'/'No, *he won't.*'

– comparative clauses (⇨ **SYNTAX 2, 5.**):
He's working much harder now than he *used to.*
I'll do as well this year as *I did* last year.

▶ Note that positive contractions of be, has, will, etc cannot be used in shortened sentences without additional words following:
'Is John coming?' 'Yes, *he is.*'/'No, *he isn't.*'/'No, *he's not.*'
BUT NOT 'Yes, he's.'

She's stronger than *I am/*than *she's ever been.*
BUT NOT She's stronger than I'm.

3. Modal Auxiliaries

■ Can, may, will, shall and must are called *modals*. They are auxiliary verbs which say something about the speaker's attitude to the probability, advisability, or suitability of the event.

■ Ought to, used to, need and dare are *semi-modals*. Unless otherwise stated, they are like the modals in meaning and grammar. But in some respects they behave like main verbs (⇨ **3.8**).

3.1 Forms

■ The modals have no -s forms, -ing forms or past participles. They are unique in using a single form throughout the present tense:

I *can* go. You *can* go. He *can* go. We *can* go. They *can* go.

■ Only four of the modals have past tense forms (but these are not just true past tenses ⇨ **3.2**).

can → could ⌐ may → might
will → would ⌐ shall → should

■ All the modals (except **may**) have contracted forms before **not**. Will, would, shall and should also have positive contracted forms (⇨ **2.7**).

3.2 The modals and tense

■ The modals do not possess the normal range of tenses. The missing tenses are often supplied by other constructions, e.g.

I can afford a car now. → **I'll soon *be able to* afford a car.**

■ The past tense forms of the modals act as true past tenses mainly in **that** clauses and especially in reported speech:

He said that he *would* come.
I asked whether I *might* use the telephone.

However, **could** can sometimes act as the past of **can** elsewhere (⇨ **3.3**).

■ Otherwise the past tense forms have special meanings of their own. They often suggest either greater uncertainty or greater politeness than the present forms, e.g.

I *may* see them tomorrow. (it's possible)
I *might* see them tomorrow. (it's less likely)

***Can* I have some more soup?**
***Could* I have some more soup?** (more polite)

3.3 *Can* and *could*

1. Can and could are used to express ability, whether learned or natural:

> **Barry *can* play the saxophone.**
> **At one time I *could* run 100 metres in 11 seconds.**

2. Can and could are used to express and ask for permission, given for example by custom or law (compare may 1.):

> **The doctor says I *can* go back to work on Monday.**
> **Can you smoke in cinemas in Britain?**

3. In questions, can is used to inquire about willingness or to ask a favour. Could is used when you want to be especially polite:

> **Can you tell me the way to the station?**
> **Could your daughter help me decorate the church?**

4. Can is used to express a possibility that is imaginable rather than actual (compare may 2.). Could shows greater doubt than can:

> **People *can* be very cruel sometimes.**
> **You *cannot* be serious!**
> **Perhaps Anne *could* take you in her car.**
> **If I had enough money, I *could* give up work.**

5. With verbs of perception like hear, see and understand there is little difference between can and the simple present tense:

> **I *can't/don't* understand what you're talking about.**

■ Can exists only in the present tense. The missing tenses can be made up using the expression be able to:

> **I *can't* do it now, but maybe I'll *be able to* on Sunday.**
> **I have never *been able to* understand him.**

Another alternative is the verb manage:

> **He was able to mend the car**
> **= He *managed* to mend the car.**

■ Could is however used as the past tense of can with a factual sense (= 'was able to and did'). In positive sentences it usually generalizes about abilities, permission, or possibilities:

> **At my last job I *could* take holidays whenever I wanted to.**
> **Ten years ago you *could* buy a house like that for £30,000.**

In negative sentences it can also refer to possibility on a single and specific past occasion:

> **I *couldn't* get any more tickets, I'm afraid.**

3.4 *May* and *might*

1. May is used to give permission when the speaker has the power to give that permission. In questions, may is used to ask permission of the person who has the power to give it. Compare can 2., must 1.

> **You *may* stay up late this evening, children.**

You *may* not smoke in here. (= You must not smoke in here.)
May I ask a question?

Might is rare in this sense except in subordinate clauses:

I asked him if I *might* borrow his hammer.

May is restricted to the present tense. Expressions such as be allowed to are used to supply the other tenses:

She *wasn't allowed to* see him again.
I hope that I'll *be allowed to* drive.

2. May is used to express a real or actual possibility. Might shows greater uncertainty than may:

For all I know, you *may* be right.
If you phone now, you *might* catch him in his office.

Compare

• •

Compare may and can 4.:

This watch can be broken.
= It is possible to break this watch.

This watch may be broken.
= It is possible that this watch has been broken.

• •

3.5 *Will* and *would*

1. Will is used to show future time, and would to show future in the past (⟹ **Verbs 2, 3.10**).

2. Will very often contains the idea of 'willingness'. Would is used in this sense chiefly in subordinate clauses:

He'*ll* carry those suitcases for you if you ask him.
He said he'*d* carry my suitcases.

Sentences with first-person subjects can therefore be interpreted as promises or statements of intention. Shall can also be used:

I'*ll* deal with this straight after lunch.
We *won't* make any noise.

In questions with second-person subjects, will usually indicates a request. Would is used for extra politeness:

'*Will* you lend me £5?' 'No, I *won't*.'
Will/Would you cook the dinner this evening?

Will is also used to give invitations or offers of help etc. Such invitations and offers are usually accepted or answered with will:

If you have any problems, I'*ll* help you.
'I'm having a party. *Will* you come?' 'Sorry, I *won't* be able to.'

Won't shows refusal or unwillingness. In this sense wouldn't can act as a past tense ('wasn't willing'):

I *won't* listen to such lies and nonsense.
He *wouldn't* tell me where he'd been.

3. Will is used to make predictions and guesses about present as well as future events. Would shows less certainty than will:

'Who's ringing the doorbell?' 'That*'ll* be the postman.'
I suppose the woman next to her *would* be her sister.

4. Would occurs in certain fixed expressions such as would like, would love, would rather:

'*Would* you like a cup of tea?' 'I*'d* love one.'
I know I've got an exam, but I*'d* rather not think about it.

Other than with the specific meanings shown, would occurs mainly in subordinate clauses, especially that and if clauses (⟹ **Syntax 2, 4.**):

I thought they*'d* lose the match.
If he took the bus, he*'d* get there quicker.

3.6 *Shall* and *should*

Shall is quite rare, especially in American English; shan't is even rarer. Should acts as the past of shall chiefly in subordinate clauses, especially in reported speech.

In the first person, shall may be used to indicate future time and should to show future in the past (⟹ **Verbs 2, 3.10**). Otherwise, the two words are used in different ways and have specific meanings of their own:

Shall

In questions with first-person subjects, shall is used to make offers, invitations, and suggestions, or to consult people:

Shall I make you a cup of tea?
Shall we go for a picnic on Sunday?

Should

1. Should (= ought to 1.) is used to give advice or to point out someone's duty:

You *should* read this book. It's very interesting.
Motorists *shouldn't* smoke while driving.

2. Should (= ought to 2.) is used to talk about strong probability:

I wonder where they are. They *should* be here by now.
There *shouldn't* be any problem getting tickets.

3. Should can be used after first-person subjects in the kinds of fixed expressions mentioned in would 6.:

I *should* like a holiday.
'Do you agree with her?' 'I *should* think so.'

4. Should is used in a variety of subordinate clauses, especially that clauses (⟹ **Syntax 2**), to introduce imagined situations. After certain verbs it acts as a sort of subjunctive:

I'm amazed that you *should* think that.

They demanded that he *should* repay the money.

Should also occurs in if clauses (⟹ **Syntax 2, 4.3**) and makes the condition seem more doubtful. This usage is rather formal:

If you *should* see him, please tell him the news.

3.7 *Must*

1. Must expresses obligation or compulsion. It is equivalent to have got to:

You *must* wear your best clothes to the interview.
I *must* get up early tomorrow morning.

The use of must and have got to is strictly limited. In this sense they are not usually used in questions, and cannot be used for repeated or habitual events. In addition, must does not have a past tense. Have to or need to are used in places where must cannot be used:

Do I *have to* wear my best clothes to the interview?
I *have to* get up early every morning to get to work.
I *needed to* get up early the following day.

The negative of must means 'it is essential not to' (= may not):

You *must not* get up early tomorrow. You *must* stay in bed.

The negatives of have to, have got to and need are used for the meaning 'it is not essential to':

Tomorrow is a holiday, so I *needn't/don't have to* get up early.

2. Must is used to show that something is logically necessary (= have got to):

It *can't* be true. I *must* be dreaming.
There *must* be some mistake.

As with sense 1., this use of must and have got to is strictly limited. They are not used in the past – have to is used instead; and in questions and negative sentences they are usually replaced by can:

It *had to* be true.
***Can* it be true?**
It *can't* be true.

Compare

• •

There is sometimes a difference between must and have got to. Must is used when the obligation comes from the speaker himself/herself; have got to is used when the obligation comes from someone else or from some other set of circumstances. Compare the following sentences:

   a. **I really *must* start going to bed earlier.** (= *personal choice*)

   b. **I've *got to* go to bed early tonight, as I'm catching the train at six a.m.** (= *external necessity*)

   c. **She says I've *got to* go to bed early tonight.** (= *external authority*)

• •

3.8 The semi-modals

Ought to

■ **Ought to** shares the meanings of **should** 1. (advice) and 2. (probability) (⇨ **3.6**). Ought to is often felt to be more objective than should, and is more common when talking about laws. When it is used to give advice, it is stronger than **should**:

1. **You *ought to* read this book. It's very interesting.**
   Motorists *ought not to* smoke while driving.
2. **I wonder where they are. They *ought to* be here by now.**

■ In informal speech the negative is often didn't ought to:

He *oughtn't to* be so rude
= He *didn't ought to* be so rude.

■ In questions and shortened sentences **ought to** usually acts like a modal, but it is not usually used in tag questions (⇨ **Syntax 1, 4.5**).

Ought we to know about this for the exam?
'I'm going home.' 'I don't think you *ought (to)*.'

Used to

■ **Used to** is used for repeated habits or long-term conditions which were once true but are not any more.

He *used to* drink too much.
I *used to* know her when I was at school.

■ The negative can be either used not to (rarely usedn't to) or didn't use(d) to. In questions used to usually acts as a main verb.

I *used not to* be so fat
= I *didn't use(d) to* be so fat.
Did he really *use(d) to* be a footballer?

■ Used to is used in some shortened sentences but usually not in tag questions (⇨ **Syntax 1, 4.5**):

I like her much more now than I *used to*.
She *used to* go out with your brother, didn't she?

Compare

● ●

Be careful not to confuse used to ['ju:st tə] with:

1. be used to + -ing form = 'be accustomed to':
   I don't mind. I'm *used to* getting up early.
2. The passive of the verb use [ju:z] + to infinitive, expressing purpose or intention:
   This part is *used to* increase the speed of the engine.

● ●

Need

■ Need is used as a modal only in questions and negative sentences, and only in the present tense. In questions it means the same as must 1.

Need we finish the work today?

■ In negative sentences it corresponds in meaning to both must 1. and must 2. But mustn't means 'it is necessary not to', while needn't means 'it is not necessary to':

You *needn't* get up early tomorrow.
That *needn't* be true.

■ In most other cases need acts like as a main verb (+ to):

We *need* to get up early tomorrow/every day.
Did you *need* to speak to me?
Your watch *needed* to be repaired, didn't it?

▶ Note also the construction + -ing:

My car needs washing = My car needs to be washed.

Dare

■ Dare can act like a modal in questions in the present tense, and in negative sentences in both present and past:

Dare I tell her that I love her?
How *dare* you speak to me like that?
I *daren't* think about it.

There is no contracted form in the past:

Tommy *dared* not go home.

■ In other cases dare is usually used as a main verb:

That rude man *dared* to call me 'darling'.
Tommy *didn't dare* go home.

Had better

Had better, like should 1. and ought to 1., is used to give advice. It sometimes has the idea of a threat or warning:

You'd better *not* do that again. She'll be very angry.

3.9 The modals and the progressive

The modals can be followed by be + the -ing form of the verb. The meaning simply combines that of the modal and that of the progressive (⇨ **2.3**):

He can't still be working. (very unlikely)
I must be dreaming. (very likely)
She will probably be having lunch when you call. (fairly certain)

3.10 The modals and the perfect tense

■ All the modals – in some of their senses at least – can be followed by (not +) have + a past participle. Most of these constructions can be interpreted in two ways (the two ways being parallel to the distinction made in past-tense if clauses, see **Syntax 2, 4.**):

1. They can be 'open' (i.e. express uncertainty) as to whether the event took place or not. Take the sentence:

> **I'm not sure, but I think you *may* have made a mistake.**

The speaker (at present) is in doubt as to whether (in the past) 'you' made a mistake or not. Using **might** instead of **may** in this sentence simply shows greater uncertainty.

Other examples of this type:

> **I *can't/couldn't* have been paying attention.**
> **He *might have* told me, but I don't remember.**
> **They *should probably have* finished work by now.**

Examples with will (⇨ **3.5**) and must (⇨ **3.7**) + have are similar, except that the speaker is expressing strong probability rather than a doubt.

> **That *will/must have* been Jenny that you saw.**
> **She *must have* forgotten to come.**

2. They can be 'hypothetical' or 'imaginary' – the speaker feels that some event in the past was possible, even though it did not in fact take place.

> **You were very lucky. You *might have* been killed** (but you weren't).
> **I *would have* liked to come but I couldn't.**
> **They *should have* finished the job yesterday.**

With needn't the event is considered unnecessary rather than merely possible:

> **You *needn't have* come if you didn't want to** (but you did).

■ Will/would and shall/should + have are also used to form compound future tenses (⇨ **Verbs 2, 3.3**) and in imaginary if sentences (⇨ **Syntax 2, 4.**):

> **I'll *have* left for America by this time tomorrow.**
> **He said that he *would have* seen her by six o'clock.**
> **I *would have* been much happier if you had told me earlier.**

■ Could + have. Could have is used like the other modals + have in both open and hypothetical senses:

Open sense:

> **I *could (= might) perhaps have* left it on the bus.**

Hypothetical sense:

> **You *could have* asked her while she was here** (but you didn't).

4. Phrasal and Prepositional Verbs

> Agnes *turned up* late.
> He's very ill. I hope he *pulls through*.
> She *turned off* the tap. She *turned* the tap *off*.
> You can *rely on* me. I'll *look after* you.
> Isn't she the girl who's *going out with* your brother?

■ Many main verbs in English are made up of two (or three) parts: a verb + one or more particles. Particles are either:
 – prepositions: for, with or into
 – adverbs, or words that are used as adverbs and prepositions: back, down, up

You have to take all the parts together to understand the meaning:

> He told me. He told me off.

■ These 'multi-word' verbs are very common in English and the language is always producing new ones. Like other verbs, they can either be intransitive, i.e. without an object, as in turn up and pull through (the first two examples above); or transitive, i.e. with an object (as in the other examples).

Intransitive multi-word verbs

The particle is usually an adverb of place. In almost all cases it follows directly after the verb:

> Please *sit down* here.
> The house *blew up*.
> The plane *took off*.
> I tried several times before finally *giving up*.

Transitive multi-word verbs

There are three types of construction in which a verb is followed by a particle + object. When the object is a noun, all three can look the same:

1. Phrasal Verbs:

> The speaker *got* his message *over* to his audience.
> (= 'communicated')

2. Prepositional Verbs:

> The company *got over* its financial problems.
> (= 'overcame')

3. Literal Verbs:

> The burglar *got over* the garden wall.
> (= 'climbed over')

These constructions have many features in common, e.g. they can all be made passive (⇨ **Verbs 3, 3.**):

> The message was *got over* clearly to the audience.
> The company's problems have now been finally *got over*.

The wall is so high that it cannot be *got over*.

However there are grammatical differences between phrasal verbs and the other two types.

4.1 Transitive phrasal verbs

> turn off (a light) ⸱ drink up (your milk)
> make up (a story) ⸱ bring up (a child)
> hold down (a job) ⸱ hold up (a bank)
> put in (an application)
> find out (some information)

■ When the object is a noun it can go either before or after the particle:

> I *made* the story *up*. I *made up* the story.

■ When it is a pronoun, it always goes before the particle:

> I *made* it *up*.

Except for objects, the only thing that can go between the verb and the particle is an adverb that qualifies the meaning of the particle.

> He *turned* the tap completely *off/on*.

■ The particle remains after the verb in questions and relative clauses (⇨ SYNTAX **1, 2. & 4.**):

> What did you *find out*?
> This is a piece of work which you must *see through* on your own.

4.2 Prepositional verbs

> look at (a picture) ⸱ ask for (some money)
> make for (the door) ⸱ refer to (a book)
> go into (a subject) ⸱ keep to (a promise)
> look over (a new house) ⸱ see through (a lie)

■ The object always goes after the particle, regardless of whether it is a noun or a pronoun:

> I *looked at* the picture. I *looked at* it.

■ The verb and the particle can be separated by adverbs etc:

> I *went carefully over* all my notes before the exam.

■ In questions and relative clauses two constructions are possible. In the first, prepositional verbs are treated like phrasal verbs; this is by far the commoner method. The second type is used only in formal English:

> *Who* are you *thinking about*?
> *About whom* are you *thinking*? *(formal)*
> The book *(which/that)* you're looking for is not available.
> The book *for which you are looking* is not available. *(formal)*

In short, prepositional verbs act like literal verbs such as **walk across** (the road), sit in (a chair), go down (the street). But –

Compare

●●●

She came across some old papers.
→ What did she *come across?*
She came across the garden.
→ Where did she *come?*

●●●

4.3 Verbs with two particles

put up with (discomfort)
look forward to (a holiday)
keep up with (one's work)
check up on (a fact)
look down on (poor people)
get away with (a crime)

■ In verbs with two particles the second particle is always a preposition. The first particle almost always follows directly after the verb; the second acts like the particle in prepositional verbs:

I hope you'll *make up with* her soon.
I *look forward* greatly *to* their arrival.
He's someone *with* whom it's impossible to *get on* well.

4.4 Other verbal idioms

■ English uses a wide variety of other combinations of a verb + other words where the meaning is more than the sum of the parts. Many of them require the use of the correct forms of the determiners my, your, etc.

In the following examples, the invariable part of these idioms is shown in italic:

I'm sorry I broke your watch but I'll *make it up* to you.
Can you *give* me *a hand* with these cases?
He was unable to *come to terms with* his job.
Don't hurry. *Take* your *time over* it.
If you don't *take care*, you'll *get* yourself *into trouble*.
Seeing a policeman there *put* me *on* my *guard*.
I've tried to forget Roger but I can't *get* him *off* my *mind*.

Many of these constructions can be made passive, e.g.

They *took* great *care* of us.
Great *care was taken* of us.
We *were taken* great *care* of.

5. The Complementation of Verbs

They *told us to stop annoying* them.
Would you *like to go out with* me this evening?
I *insist on speaking to* the manager.
She *saw him steal* the apples.

Many verbs can be followed by other verbs, as in the examples above. The first verb decides which form the second verb will have. Good dictionaries supply this information.

5.1 Verb + verb constructions

a. *Verb + base form*. The modals (⇨ **3.**) and auxiliary do are followed directly by the base form of the verb:

You *should buy* yourself some new shoes.
Didn't they warn you about the crocodiles?

b. *Verb + to + base form*, e.g. want, refuse:

Do you *want to know* a secret?
She *refused to listen* to me.

Some common verbs which are followed by to + base form:

afford	agree	appear
arrange	ask	attempt
bear	beg	begin
care	choose	consent
dare	decide	determine
expect	fail	forget
happen	hate	help
hesitate	hope	intend
learn	manage	mean
neglect	offer	prepare
pretend	promise	propose
refuse	regret	seem
start	swear	trouble
try	want	wish

c. *Verb + -ing form*, e.g. enjoy, stop:

It's *stopped raining*.
Do you *enjoy reading* long novels?

Some common verbs which are followed by the -ing form:

admit	appreciate	avoid
consider	delay	deny
detest	dislike	enjoy
excuse	finish	forgive
give up	hate	can't help
imagine	keep	mind
miss	practise	put off
resist	risk	seem
start	suggest	understand

■ The verb **go** + -ing form is particularly common in the sense of to take part in some recreational activity:

> I often *go dancing/drinking/running/shooting*, etc.

It contrasts with the simple verb:

> **I like swimming.** (= I like to swim.)
> **I like going swimming.** (= I like being at the swimming pool.)

■ Some verbs can be followed by either to + base form or the -ing form, e.g. like, hate, prefer, intend, plan, try, start. There is generally little difference in meaning: to + base form tends to be used for single events, the -ing form for repeated events:

> **I *hate to tell* a lie, but this time perhaps it's necessary.**
> **I *hate telling* lies. It always makes me feel bad.**

Compare

•••

With remember and forget there is a very clear difference between the *verb + to + base form* and the *verb + -ing form*:

> **I *remembered to post* your letter.**
> **I *remembered posting* your letter.**

With stop the difference is even more marked:

> **He *stopped to smoke*.** (= He stopped walking in order to have a cigarette.)
> **He *stopped smoking*.** (= He gave up smoking.)

•••

d. *Verb + preposition + -ing form*, e.g. insist on, keep on, believe in, boast about, delight in, leave off, be tired of, look forward to. These are really prepositional verbs (⟹ **4.2**).

> **She *insisted on paying* for the meal.**
> **I wish he'd *refrain from smoking*.**

┌ Note ──────────────────────────

In informal speech, try and go are often followed by and + the base form:

> **I'll *go and* see what's happening outside.**
> **Please *try and* keep yourself warm.**

5.2 Verb + object + verb constructions

Many verbs can have an object before a following verb:

a. *Verb + object + base form*, e.g. let, make, see, hear, help:

> **She *lets her children do* what they like.**
> **Please *make yourself look* a little tidier.**
> **I *saw Frank take* your newspaper.**

b. *Verb + object + to + base form*, e.g. ask, allow, expect, tell, persuade, get (= 'make'), want, invite, remind, believe:

Clare *asked her manager to give* her a pay rise.
I *want you to try* to persuade him to come.
We *believed him to be* lying.

c. *Verb + object + -ing form*, e.g. prefer, remember, can't stand, hate, oppose, start, stop, see, hear, help, find:

I *can't stand people swearing* in public.
We *found our dog digging* up the flowers.

Note

In formal English, the object can be in the possessive form after some of these verbs:

David said he *enjoyed you/your singing* to them.
I *dislike John/John's laughing* at me.

■ Some verbs – mostly verbs of perception – can be followed by an object and either the base form alone or to + base form, e.g. see, hear, find. There is generally little difference in meaning:

I heard them *come up* the stairs.
I heard them *coming up* the stairs.

■ Others can be followed by an object and either to + base form or the -ing form, e.g. like, hate, prefer. Generally, there is little difference in meaning: to + base form tends to be used for single events, the -ing form for repeated events:

Would you *like me to read* to you?
I *like you reading* to me.

d. *Verb + object + preposition + -ing form* of verbs, e.g. prevent from, stop from, thank for, blame for, interest in, congratulate on:

I don't *blame you for getting* angry.
Clive's parents *prevented him from joining* the army.

e. *Verb + preposition + object + -ing form* of verbs, e.g. insist on, believe in, boast about, delight in, be tired of, look forward to. In formal English the object can be in the possessive form:

The librarian *insisted on us/our being* quiet.
I'm really *tired of my mother/mother's nagging* me.

f. *Verb + object + past participle*, e.g. have, get, see, hear, find. The meaning is always partly passive:

Have you had your hair coloured?
I came back and *found the money stolen.*

■ Passive forms. Some of the verbs using constructions a.–d. can be made passive (⇨ **Verbs 3, 3.**). Those in type a. above add to (i.e. like those in b.):

We were *made to do* the cleaning.
She can't be *persuaded to come.*
The children were *heard laughing and playing* about.
I was *congratulated on winning* the tournament.

■ Complementation by clauses. Many verbs can only have full clause complements, e.g. say, decide, demand:

She *decided that it was* a good idea.
I *wonder why he did* it.

Others can be followed by either full clauses or object + verb constructions:

I *believe that he is* a liar. = I *believe him to be* a liar.

▶ With others, especially those which take a preposition + -ing form, only the Verb + Object + Verb construction is possible. Foreign learners often make the mistake of using that clauses after verbs where this is not possible:

I *want you to get* the job.   **I *object to you spitting.***
NOT **I want that you get the job.**   *NOT* **I object that you spit.**

Verbs 2

1. Actions in the Present
I take . I am taking
2. Actions in the Past
I took . I was taking . I have taken
3. Actions in the Future
I will take . I'm going to take

1. Actions in the Present

■ English has two main verb forms showing that an event or condition is true at the present:

– *The simple present tense*: this is used chiefly for repeated events, customs, habits, and long-term states:

> **My brother *works* in an insurance office.**
> ***Do* you *know* Kate Harrison?**

– *The present progressive tense*: this is used chiefly for events restricted to a limited period of time including the present moment:

> **Chelsea *are winning* 2-0 with ten minutes left.**
> ***Is* your car *working* properly now?**

▶ Note that the progressive or 'continuous' combines with other tenses, e.g. past and future. All these compound tenses have much in common. You will understand the present progressive better if you understand the meaning of the progressive in general (⇨ **1.8**):

> **I *was* just *leaving* when the telephone rang.**
> **They*'ve been playing* golf a lot recently.**

It is also important to know when the progressive cannot be used (⇨ **1.9**):

> **These shoes don't fit me.**
> *NOT* **These shoes aren't fitting me.**

1.1 The simple present: forms

	Singular	Plural
1st person	I *like* music.	We *like* music.
2nd person	You *like* music.	You *like* music.
3rd person	He/she/it *likes* music.	They *like* music.

Irregular forms
The verb be (⇨ **Verbs 1, 2.2**):

> **I am; you/we/they are; he/she/it is**

The modals (⇨ **Verbs 1, 3.**), e.g.

> I can, he can; I must, she must.

■ The third person singular -s form is described fully in **Verbs 1, 1.2**.

■ Question, negative and emphatic forms require the use of auxiliaries (⇨ **Verbs 1, 2.**). Since the simple present has no auxiliaries, the appropriate forms of the auxiliary do are used:

> *Do I (you/we/they) finish* at 8 o'clock?
> *Does he (she/it) finish* at 8 o'clock?
> I (you/we/they) *don't like* milk.
> He (she/it) *doesn't like* milk.
> You needn't worry. She *does* believe you.

> Note that in rapid speech, do you is pronounced [dju:] or [dʒu:].

1.2 The simple present: meaning

> I *live* in Glasgow but I *work* in Edinburgh.
> *Do* you *remember* her sister's name?
> Andy *plays* football.

■ The meaning of the simple present depends partly on the kind of verb it is used with:

– With verbs describing states or conditions, the simple present shows what is always true:

> Jenny *likes* chocolate.
> *Do* you *think* they'll agree?
> Two *times* three *makes* six.
> *Does* the Thames *flow* through Oxford?

– With verbs describing actions or events, the simple present shows that the event is habitual, customary, or repeated. The action is not necessarily happening now. This usage is often accompanied by adverbs of time, such as always, often, sometimes, occasionally, never:

> He *plays* tennis on Saturdays.
> *Don't* you ever *eat* meat?
> It *rains* a lot in Wales.

1.3 Other uses of the simple present

■ After I or we, the simple present of verbs like promise, refuse, wish, and accept 'performs the action' described in the sentence:

> I'm sorry. I *beg* your pardon.
> We *wish* you every success in your exams.

■ The simple present of verbs like hear, understand, say, claim can repeat recent information which is still valid:

> I *hear* that you've lost your purse.
> The weather forecast *says* that it's going to rain today.

■ In dramatic situations like sports commentaries, the simple present can describe sudden events as they actually happen. It is also used for giving instructions and demonstrations:

Robson *passes* to McLair. McLair *shoots*, and it's a goal!
You *put* two eggs into a bowl and *add* 200 grams of flour.

This use is occasionally transferred to past events to make them appear more vivid, for example in newspaper headlines or when telling a joke:

A man *goes* into a pub and *asks* for a pint of beer ...

Under newspaper photograph:
Mitterrand *shakes* hands with Kohl.

■ The simple present can have a future meaning, especially in if and when clauses (⇨ **3.7**):

He'll get into trouble if he *carries* on like that.
She'll see her mother again when she *goes* to London next month.

■ See **1.9** for verbs which cannot usually be used in the progressive. In such cases, the simple present is used to talk about temporary situations:

I like your coat.
NOT **I am liking your coat.**

1.4 The progressive: general meaning

The commonest use of the progressive is to talk about an action or situation that covers a period before (and after) the main time of the sentence. Though extended, this period is usually limited or short-term. In the following sentence, the main time is the past:

They arrived while we were washing the dishes.

The times of the two actions can be viewed as follows:

TIME

We were washing the dishes `- - - - - - - - - - - - - - - - - - ➤`
They arrived   ✗

Compare

● ●

Note that the following sentences do not mean the same:

When Jane got home her husband *was making* the dinner.
When Jane got home her husband *made* the dinner.

The first says that Jane's husband was already preparing the food before she got home; the second says that he did not start until after she got home.

● ●

■ When two extended events overlap, the progressive can be used in both clauses:

> You *were watching* the television while I *was washing* up.

■ With the present progressive, the time of the action covers the moment of speaking:

> Shut up. I'*m trying* to think.

For the progressive with different types of verbs, see **1.8**. For a special use of the future continuous, see **3.3 & 3.4**.

1.5 The present progressive: forms

> Be quiet. I'*m listening* to the radio.
> *Are* you all *sitting* comfortably?

■ The present progressive uses the present tense of the verb be + the -ing form of the main verb (⇨ **VERBS 1, 1.**). In questions the subject is placed after the auxiliary (⇨ **VERBS 1, 2.**):

> *Is your mother making* the dinner?

■ In negative sentences, not is added after the auxiliary. In speech one usually uses contracted forms (⇨ **VERBS 1, 2.7**):

> Our company is doing well.
> → Our company *isn't* doing well.
> → Our company'*s* not doing well.

▶ Note that the second type of contraction is not possible when the subject is I:

> I'*m not* feeling very well.

1.6 The present progressive: meanings

■ The present progressive is used for events which go on for a limited period of time covering the present moment. The event has already started; it need not be complete.

> 'What'*s happening*?' 'We'*re* just *going* out.'

For the present progressive with future meaning, see **3.5**:

> I'*m starting* work at the bakery on Monday.

■ The meaning of the present progressive depends largely on the kind of verb it is used with:

– With verbs describing activities, the progressive suggests that the activity is actually happening now:

> It'*s raining*.
> You'*re talking* too loud.
> She'*s wearing* a white blouse and a blue skirt.

– With verbs describing sudden or instantaneous actions, the progressive suggests that the action is repeated several times:

> The children *are jumping* up and down with happiness.

Please, teacher, Billy Smith*'s hitting* me.
– With verbs describing changes in state or condition, the progressive suggests an approach towards that condition:

The bus *is stopping* at the bus stop.
They*'re widening* the pavement down the road.

These interpretations also apply to the progressive used with other tenses (⇨ **1.8**).

Remember that some verbs are not used with the progressive at all (⇨ **1.9**).

1.7 Simple present v. present progressive

'**What do you do?**' '**I work in a bank.**'
'**What are you doing?**' '**I'm cleaning my room.**'

In general, as in these examples, there is a clear difference between the 'long-term' simple present and the 'short-term' present progressive. Note the following contrasts:

■ The present progressive can be used for states and conditions when their duration is limited. Compare the following pairs:

We *live* in Leeds. (Leeds is our permanent home.)
We*'re living* in Leeds. (Leeds is our temporary home.)
Our car *runs* well. (i.e. in general)
Our car *is running* well. (at this moment, or for the time being)

■ Habits which are only temporary can be described with the present progressive even if the action is not actually happening now:

You*'re smoking* far too much these days.
I*'m taking* the train to work while my car's being fixed.

■ Other kinds of repeated events can be described with the present progressive but only when they are seen as temporary (compare **1.2**):

People *are arriving* every ten minutes.
Every time I see him he*'s wearing* the same coat.

■ The present progressive, especially combined with **always** or **forever**, is used even for longer-term habits to give the sentence a critical tone:

He*'s always* complaining about his boss.
They*'re forever coming* to us with their problems.

The simple present of the verb **keep** conveys a similar meaning:

She *keeps phoning* me up and asking stupid questions.

■ When talking about physical feelings, there is little difference between the simple present and the present progressive:

How do you feel now? = How are you feeling now?
My head hurts a bit. = My head is hurting a bit.

1.8 The progressive with other tenses

The progressive can combine with all the other tenses by using the
appropriate form of auxiliary be + the -ing form of the main verb,
e.g.:

– with the past tense (⇨ **2.4**):

> We *were playing* chess when the phone rang.
> I *was working* from morning till night.

– with the present perfect (⇨ **2.6**):

> I've *been thinking* of buying some new shoes.
> He's *been seeing* her a lot recently.

– with the future (⇨ **3.3**):

> They'll *be working* all next week.
> Don't call before six. We'll *be doing* the shopping.

■ Remember that:

– in questions the auxiliary precedes the subject (⇨ **Verbs 1, 2.8**):
> Why *were* your friends driving so fast?
> When *will* they be leaving?

– in negative sentences, not is placed after the first auxiliary:
> We *weren't* expecting you to phone.
> I *haven't* been feeling very well for the last few days.

– in speech contracted forms are usually used (⇨ **Verbs 1, 2.7**):
> We'll be home by nine.

1.9 Limitations in the use of the progressive

■ Some verbs are never used in the progressive; others are only used
in the progressive in certain senses.

■ Certain verbs which indicate some long-term state or condition are
not normally used in the progressive:

– Verbs of natural perception (rather than perception made by
effort), e.g. feel, hear, see, smell, sound, taste. These verbs often
follow can:
> I *can see* you. NOT I am seeing you.

– Verbs describing mental states or understanding, e.g. believe,
remember, imagine, know, suppose, understand, doubt, guess,
mean, realize, recognize:
> Do *you believe* in God?
> NOT Are you believing in God?

– Verbs describing mental attitudes, e.g. like, hate, prefer, want,
wish, hope, think, consider:
> Bob *loves* Sue. NOT Bob is loving Sue.

– Verbs describing long-term 'having' or 'being', e.g. be (usually),
belong to, own, consist of, cost, depend on, matter, resemble,
appear, include, lack, possess:

Are you **okay?** *NOT* **Are you being okay?**
That *seems* **to be right.** *NOT* **That is seeming to be right.**
These shoes *don't fit* **me.** *NOT* **These shoes aren't fitting me.**
The box *contains* **sweets.** *NOT* **The box is containing sweets.**

■ However, some adjectives and nouns do allow the progressive after be:

The children *are being* **naughty.**
My brother's *being* **a nuisance again.**

■ Meaning alone does not always tell you whether a verb can or cannot be used in the progressive. This has to be learned for each verb separately. For instance, the first of these sentences is properly formed, the second is not:

We *are enjoying* **our holiday.** *NOT* **We are liking our holiday.**

■ Many verbs which do not allow the progressive in the simple tenses can be used in compound progressive tenses:

I *need* **a hammer.** *NOT* **I am needing a hammer.**
BUT: **Can you lend me your tools. I'***ll be needing* **a hammer tomorrow.**

■ Many verbs have distinct meanings depending on whether they are used in the progressive or not. For example, those verbs like **feel, hear, see** mentioned in the first group above:

Compare:

The soup *tastes* **wonderful.**
The cook *is tasting* **the soup.**
I *(can) see* **some ships.**
I'*m seeing* **her soon.** (= meeting)
I *think* **you're wrong.** (= believe)
I'*m thinking* **of getting a dog.** (= considering)

▶ There are two main verbs **have** in English:

1. = 'own, possess, etc'. This verb does not have a progressive and can be replaced by **have got**:

I have (got) £10/red hair/a sister/influenza.

2. = 'make, experience'. This verb has a progressive and cannot be replaced by **have got**:

We're having breakfast/a bath/a rest/a good time/an examination/trouble.

See also **VERBS 1, 2.1**.

2. Actions in the Past

■ English uses a number of tenses to speak of events that have already taken place. The two most important are:

– *The simple past tense:* the event or state described is felt to be completely finished:

Billy *stole* the apples yesterday.

– *The present perfect tense:* the event or state happened before now but is felt to be still relevant:

Billy *has stolen* the apples and hidden them.

■ Both the simple past and the perfect can combine with other tenses, e.g. the progressive:

Past progressive (⇨ **2.4**):

I *was driving* all day yesterday.

Present perfect progressive (⇨ **2.11**):

I*'ve been driving* all day and still have 100 miles to go.

■ The perfect is used with other tenses to push the events described back to before the main time of the sentence (⇨ **2.10**):

Past Perfect: **They *had gone* by the time I arrived.**

Future Perfect: **We *will have eaten* before you arrive.**

These tenses also combine with the progressive (⇨ **2.11**).

2.1 The simple past tense: forms

I *slept* badly because the bed was uncomfortable.
He *seemed* to be unhappy about something.
We *were* very worried. Why *didn't* you *phone*?

■ Positive statements are made using the past tense form. The past tense form is invariable except for the verb be (⇨ **Verbs 1, 1. & 2.**): I/he/she/it was; you/we/they were.

I *knew* him when I *was* young.
Jenny *asked* us whether we *were* happy.

■ Questions, negatives and emphatic forms require the use of auxiliaries. Since the simple past has no auxiliaries, the auxiliary did is used (⇨ **Verbs 1, 2.**). Compare the simple present (⇨ **1.1**):

– Questions

Did you remember to feed the cat?

In rapid speech, did you is usually pronounced ['dɪdʒuː].

– Negatives. See **Verbs 1, 2.7** for negative contractions.

My sisters *didn't* do very well in their exams.
That *wasn't* a very good idea.

– Emphatic Forms

Now I remember! I *did* see him yesterday!

2.2 The simple past tense: meaning and usage

■ The simple past is used for events and states which are viewed as being completely finished. The speaker has some definite time in mind. How long ago that was is irrelevant:

The Earth *was* formed about 4,600 million years ago.
To doctor giving injection: **Ow, that *hurt!***

■ Stories and novels are written mainly in the simple past:

There *was* once a beautiful princess who *had* a wicked stepmother...

■ The event or condition is regarded as a single whole. The length of time, or whether the whole event was repeated many times, is irrelevant:

The Romans *invaded* Britain in 44 AD and *remained* for 400 years.
In one year Jeremy *sold* 25 cars.

■ When verbs are joined by **and**, it can be unclear whether the events happened at the same time or one after the other:

Yesterday I *tidied* my room and *listened* to some records.

■ To stress that a past event was a repeated habit, you can use an adverb such as **often** or the auxiliary used to (⟹ **Verbs 1, 3.8**):

They *used to* live just down the road.
He *often* went for walks in the evening.

■ Time indicators with the simple past: **ago** and **for**.

Ago and for: differences

Ago – *Meaning*: ago is used to say when past events happened.

> *Usage*: ago is used with the simple past tenses and answers the question 'When?'
>
> *Position*: ago follows the time adverbial:

I went to Italy *two years ago*. (When?)

For – *Meaning*: for is used to say how long past events lasted.

> *Usage*: for is used with the simple past tense or the present perfect and follows the time adverbial; and answers the question 'How long?'
>
> *Position*: for comes before the time adverbial.

I went to Italy *for three weeks*. (How long?)

Ago and before: differences

four years *ago* = four years before now (i.e. the moment of speaking)
four years *before* = four years before then (i.e. a time already mentioned in the past)
I went to New York *two years ago*.
I went to New York in 1990 with my wife. It was her first visit, but I had already been there *two years before*.

2.3 Other uses of the simple past

■ The simple past is used in certain imaginary constructions such as if clauses (⇨ **SYNTAX 2, 4.**):

If you really *loved* me you wouldn't keep criticizing my mother.
It's time that the baby *was* in bed.

■ The simple past can be used for present events when the speaker wants to be especially polite, for instance in requests. Compare the modals (⇨ **VERBS 1, 3.**):

'Did you *want* to see me?' 'Yes, I *wondered* if you could help us.'

2.4 The past progressive: form

■ The past progressive uses the past tense of the verb be + the -ing form of the verb:

I *was watching* the television when you called.
One of them *was working* while the rest *were drinking* their coffee.
She *was living* in Birmingham at the time.
A police spokesman said that the house *was being* watched.

■ In questions, the subject is placed after the auxiliary (⇨ **VERBS 1, 2.**):

Where were you going when I saw you?

■ In negative sentences, not is added after the auxiliary:

It wasn't raining when I left the house.

▶ Note that contractions occur between the *auxiliary* and not. Contractions between the *subject* and *auxiliary* are only possible in the present progressive:

It's not raining. (= It is not raining.)

2.5 The past progressive: meaning

■ The past progressive combines the meaning of the past with that of the progressive. It is used for events or states which continued for a limited period covering the main time of a sentence set in the past:

They *were still arguing* at the end of the meeting.

■ Often the 'main time' is only implicit, and the past progressive merely suggests that the event was extended over a limited period:

'What *were you doing* on Saturday?' 'We *were visiting* relatives.'

■ The past progressive often suggests that the event described was fairly recent. It is often used with just or recently:

I *was thinking* about buying a new car.
My sister *was just saying* that there's been a fire at her school.

■ The past progressive is sometimes used instead of the simple present in polite enquiries and requests:

> *Were you wanting* anything?
> *I was hoping* that you might be able to give me some advice.

Remember: some verbs cannot be used in the progressive (⇨ **1.9**).

2.6 The present perfect tense: form

> They*'ve painted* their house purple.
> I *have thought* about it a lot and I still don't agree.
> *Have* you ever *seen* a kangaroo?

■ The present perfect uses the present tense of the auxiliary **have** + the past participle (⇨ **Verbs 1, 1.5**). For the positive contractions of the auxiliary **have**, see **Verbs 1, 2.7**:

> I*'ve been* ill. She*'s been* ill.

■ Questions and negative sentences are formed in the usual ways for verb forms with auxiliaries (⇨ **Verbs 1, 2.**):

> *Have you studied* the past tense in English?
> *Has Ron been* to work today?
> *Why hasn't my pay gone up* this year?

Compare

• •

The verb **go** has two different past participles when used in perfect tenses: **gone** and **been**:

> The Fosters *have gone* to Spain for their holiday.
> The Fosters *have been* to Spain for their holiday.

The first sentence says that the Fosters have left for Spain and are still there; the second suggests that the Fosters were in Spain at one time but have now returned. So it is more natural to say:

> Ask Julie. She*'s been* to Mexico, so she can tell you about it.

This difference holds for the other perfect tenses, such as the past perfect:

> I couldn't see him because he*'d gone* to London.
> When I last saw him he*'d* just *been* to London.

• •

2.7 The present perfect: meaning

■ The present perfect is used for past events which are felt in some way to remain relevant in the present. The interpretation depends partly on the choice of the main verb. In each case, it is useful to compare the present perfect with the simple past (s. past):

– The present perfect with verbs describing **states** or **conditions** indicates that the state or condition still persists:

perfect: She*'s lived* in Norwich all her life (and she still does).

s. past: **She *lived* in Norwich all her life (but now she is dead).**

perfect: **I've *known* Ken since I was at school (and I still see him often).**

s. past: **I *knew* Ken when I was at school (but then he moved away).**

– It is used for habits and customs which still continue:

perfect: **She's *taught* French for twenty years (and she still does).**

s. past: **She *taught* French for twenty years (but now she is retired).**

perfect: ***Have you always spent* your Saturdays shopping?**

– It is used with verbs describing events if the results of the event are still present:

perfect: **They've *mended* the fence. Isn't that an improvement?**

s. past: **They *mended* the fence yesterday, but it's fallen down again.**

perfect: **My watch *has stopped*. (Somebody trod on it.)**

perfect: **I've *broken* my arm. (I did it on my skiing holiday.)**

– It is used with event verbs if the time of the event is felt to be less important than its present significance:

perfect: **I've *read* Macbeth (so I can tell you the story).**

s. past: **I *read* Macbeth at school (but I've forgotten all about it now).**

perfect: **We've *already had* measles (so we can't catch it again).**

perfect: ***Have you seen* my newspaper? (I want to read it.)**

■ Time indicators with the present perfect.

For and since: differences

For indicates how long something has lasted:
   I've known her *for* six years/*for* ages.
Since indicates the point when something started:
   I've known her *since* 1978/*since* we were children.

Still, yet and already: differences

Still is used to describe an action or state which is continuing:
   It's *still* raining. (continuing)
Yet is used in negatives and questions to convey certain expectations on the part of the speaker about an action or state:
   It hasn't stopped raining *yet*. (I expect it will stop eventually)
Already is used to say that something has happened earlier than the speaker expected:
   It's *already* stopped raining. (sooner than I expected)
   It's stopped raining *already*. (expresses surprise)

2.8 The 'indefinite past': present perfect v. simple past

■ The present perfect places events in the 'indefinite past'. If the speaker has a definite time in mind, the simple past tense is used:

perfect: *Have you seen* the Van Gogh exhibition at the Tate Gallery?

s. past: *Did you see* the Van Gogh exhibition, as you said you would?

■ Once an event has been mentioned it is no longer 'indefinite'. When further details are added they are usually in the past tense:

Alison has been offered the job. We *were* all very surprised.
I've only played rugby once and I *didn't* enjoy it very much.

■ The simple past views an event as a single thing; if it was repeated it is usual to say so by using the adverb often or the auxiliaries used to and would (⇨ **Verbs 1, 3.**). The present perfect is unspecific about the number of times an event occurred. So it is suitable for events that could have happened more than once, particularly if they could still happen again:

He *often stole* things from cars.
He*'s stolen* from cars before (so he might have stolen your radio).

■ By stressing the auxiliary the speaker can make it clear that although the event is finished it still has important results or relevance:

Don't nag me. I *have* washed the dishes.
Jill might know. Unlike you, she *has* studied Spanish.

2.9 Simple past and present perfect with time indicators

■ The present perfect cannot be used when a sentence contains an adverb or other time indicator which sets it firmly in the past – that is, which answers the question 'when?' – e.g. a week ago, last year, on Tuesday, at one o'clock, when I was young:

We *visited* the Science Museum yesterday.
I've just seen him. He *got* here five minutes ago.
When *did* you *speak* to them?

■ The present perfect is used if the time indicator covers the period up to and including the present – for instance, answering the question 'how long?' or 'how often?', e.g. so far, until now. The commonest such time indicators are phrases and clauses beginning with since and phrases beginning with for:

He*'s worked* at Healey's for five years/since 1989.
'How long *have you been* here?' 'I've been waiting for an hour.'

However, the past is used with time phrases beginning with for when the period is completely finished:

He *worked* at Healey's for five years during the 1980s.

■ Both the simple past and the present perfect are possible with time indicators which say 'when' but which also include the present moment, e.g. this morning, today:

> She *wrote* some postcards today (and won't write any more).
> She*'s written* some postcards today (and might write some more).

■ The present perfect is common with frequency adverbs like always, sometimes, and never; and with already, yet, recently and just.

> I*'ve always wanted* to have a surfboard.
> *Have you ever been* arrested?
> '*Have you started* the cleaning *yet?*' 'I*'ve already finished* it.'
> *Have you read* any good books *recently?*

It is also common with expressions containing numbers:

> This is the second time I've had to speak to you.
> She's called five times today.

Informal American usage often favours a simple past form where one would expect the present perfect form of the verb to be used (e.g. with time adverbs):

> I just *saw* him.
> We already *ate* our lunch.
> *Did* you ever *see* such a thing?

Compare

●●

Ever, already, yet and still are used with the present perfect in British English and with the simple past in American English:

> *Have you ever been* to France? (British)
> *Did you ever go* to France? (American)

Yet is placed at the end of the clause/sentence/question.

Still, ever and already are usually found in mid-position with the verb.

●●

2.10 Compound tenses of the perfect

■ The perfect combines with tenses other than the simple present. In most cases its effect is simply to 'push events backwards' in time before the main time of the sentence (which is usually expressed by a time adverbial, e.g. before the exams, when the fire alarm rang, by Monday, by the time you arrive). For instance:

> He*'ll have arrived* by the time you leave.

The main time of this sentence is future. By using the future perfect have arrived, the sentence makes it clear that the 'arriving' will happen before the 'leaving'.

■ The perfect appears in the following compound tenses. For the order of the auxiliaries, see **Verbs 1, 2.5**.

Present perfect progressive:
> I**'ve been sitting** here for three hours now.

Past perfect:
> I**'d been very worried** before the exams, but they went quite well.

Past perfect progressive:
> We**'d only been working** for ten minutes when the fire alarm rang.

Future perfect:
> Do they think that they**'ll have repaired** my bike by Monday?

Future perfect progressive:
> By the time you arrive I**'ll have been working** for ten hours.

2.11 The present perfect progressive

■ The present perfect progressive combines the main ideas of the perfect and progressive. It is not usually used with verbs that do not appear in the present progressive (⇨ **1.9**).

■ The present perfect progressive is used for events which have been going on for some time and whose results are still present:
> This seat's wet. It**'s been raining**.
> Your hands are dirty. What *have you been doing*?

■ It often implies that the event is not yet completed or finished. Compare the ordinary present perfect:
> Who**'s been taking** my sweets? (There are still some left.)
> Perfect:
> Who**'s taken** my sweets? (There are none left.)
> I**'ve been working** on my essay all day (and I'm still at it).
> Perfect:
> I**'ve worked** on my essay all day (and I'm finished now).

There is often an idea of 'limited duration', as is usual with the progressive (⇨ **1.5**):
> I**'ve been working** here for ten days now and I'm enjoying it.
> Perfect:
> I**'ve worked** here for ten years and I don't intend to leave.

■ The present perfect progressive is particularly common with verbs indicating temporary states such as wait, sit, stand, and stay:
> She**'s been sitting** there for hours now.
> How long *have we been waiting* for this bus?

2.12 The past perfect

■ The past perfect combines the past of the auxiliary have and the past participle:

I *had seen* the film already.

■ When the main time of the sentence is the past tense, the past perfect is used to describe events which occurred even further back in the past:

We *had* already *left* by the time Carolyn arrived.

■ The past perfect occurs often in subordinate clauses, especially in reported speech (⇨ **Syntax 2, 7.**). In such cases it acts as the past of both the simple past and the present perfect:

'Have you seen her yet?'
→ He asked me if I *had seen* her yet.
'Were you frightened?'
→ He asked me if I *had been frightened*.

■ In clauses beginning with when, after, etc it is common to use the simple past even though the past perfect seems more natural:

I saw Ben some time after I spoke to you.

■ The past perfect also has a progressive form:

He *had been sitting* there for two hours before she arrived.

3. Actions in the Future

■ English has no future tense as such. Instead, it uses a variety of present-tense forms to show that an event has yet to happen. Each of these forms has a slightly different meaning. The choice usually depends on the attitude of the speaker – how likely he/she thinks the event is, for instance, or how soon it might happen.

■ The commonest ways of indicating future time are:
– will/shall + base form:
> **They *will be* here soon.** (⇨ **3.1**)

– be going to + base form:
> **It*'s going to rain*.** (⇨ **3.4**)

– the present progressive tense:
> **She*'s taking* me out tonight.** (⇨ **3.5**)

– will/shall + be + -ing form:
> **I*'ll be going* home next week.** (⇨ **3.6**)

– the simple present tense:
> **The train *leaves* at 8 o'clock.** (⇨ **3.7**)

– be to/be about to:
> **We*'re to see* him on Tuesday.** (⇨ **3.8 & 3.9**)

English uses the past tenses of some of these forms to show future in the past, for instance in reported speech (⇨ **3.10**):
> **She said that she *would* buy me a present.**

3.1 Will/shall: forms

> **I*'ll see* you this evening.**
> **We *shan't* be there on time.**
> **Will you *send* it tomorrow?**

■ Will and shall are typical invariable modals (⇨ **Verbs 1, 3.5 & 3.6**). For the contracted positive forms (he'll, etc), and the contracted negative forms (won't, shan't), see **Verbs 1, 2.7**.

Regular form:

SUBJECT + WILL + VERB
> **I *will* go.**
> **She *will* stay.**

■ The positive contracted forms, e.g. I'll, you'll, are used for both will and shall. The form shan't is rare in all varieties of English.

■ Questions and negative sentences are formed following the usual pattern for auxiliary verbs (⇨ **Verbs 1, 2.**):
> **Will there *be* anything nice to eat?**
> **Mr Smith *won't be able* to see you before 11 o'clock.**

Negative sentences with pronoun subjects have two possible forms.

The second is more emphatic, and much less common, than the first:

They *won't be* back by this evening.
They*'ll not be* back by this evening.

▶ A very common mistake is to use will in clauses beginning with if, when, after, etc. In such clauses the verb is normally simple present even if the meaning is future (⇨ **3.7**):

We will stay at home if it *rains*.
I'll tell her when I *see* her.

■ Shall is used to indicate simple future, but only in the first person (singular and plural):

I *shall* see him tomorrow. = I will see him tomorrow.
I suppose we *shall* be late. = I suppose we will be late.

In British English, and particularly in American English, shall is now rare, however, except in suggestions (⇨ **3.2**):

***Shall* we go to the cinema this evening?**

3.2 *Will/shall*: uses

■ The main idea of will and shall can be summed up as 'prediction'; that is, they show what the speaker thinks is likely to happen. They can therefore be used fairly generally:

I*'ll be* at home tomorrow.
Where *will you be* next month?
We*'ll be* back in time for dinner.
I think that Jane *will get* the job.
By the year 2025 there *will be* no oil left.

However, they are not particularly suitable when the event is certain rather than predictable or when there is a strong idea of personal intention. In such cases the be going to form (⇨ **3.4**) or the present progressive (⇨ **3.5**) would be more usual.

■ Particularly after verbs like think, using will and shall often indicates a sudden decision about future intentions:

I think I*'ll go* for a walk.
Don't worry about that. I*'ll see* to it.

■ As well as being auxiliaries of the future, will and shall have a variety of other senses (⇨ **Verbs 1, 3.5 & 3.6**). Note that many of these senses contain an idea of the future – if you promise or are 'willing' to do something, for instance, your doing it will be in the future:

I*'ll help* you with your homework.
***Will you come* with me to the theatre tonight?**

■ In questions with first-person subjects there is sometimes a contrast between will and shall:

***Will I go* into the examination before you?**
***Shall I go* into the examination before you?**

The first example asks a question – 'Is it predictable or planned that I

The first example asks a question – 'Is it predictable or planned that I will go before you?' The second is an offer – 'If you want me to, I'll go into the examination before you.'

3.3 Compound tenses of *will* and *shall*

They*'ll be digging* up the road next week.
Will you have finished your exams by next Friday?
The part of Hamlet *will be played* by Julian Fry.

■ Will and shall can be combined with the progressive, the perfect, and the passive. The meanings are mostly predictable – those of the progressive (⇨ **1.4**), perfect (⇨ **2.6**) and passive (⇨ **VERBS 3, 3.**) moved forward into the future.

For the order of the auxiliaries, see (⇨ **VERBS 1, 2.5**).
For uses of the future progressive, see (⇨ **3.6**).

Future perfect: will/shall + have + past participle

The future perfect is used for events that will be finished before some other time or event in the future:

Celia *will* probably *have* arrived by 8 o'clock.
If we don't hurry, the plane *will have left* before we get there.

■ With clauses using if or when + the simple present, the future perfect can indicate that some new aim or total has been reached:

If we win on Saturday, *we'll have won* our last five matches.
When I finish this book, I*'ll have read* the whole list.

Future passive: will/shall + be + past participle

You *will be shot* at dawn.
This *will be dealt with* in the next chapter.

Other combinations

Sentences which use other combinations of tenses with future meaning normally include other information which indicates exactly when the future event will take place. Here are some examples:

Future perfect progressive:

By the time we get home, *we'll have been driving* for eight hours.

Future perfect passive:

The work *will* probably *have been finished* by Friday.

Future progressive passive:

You can't use the car next week. It*'ll be being repaired.*

■ The future perfect progressive often describes something that the speaker thinks may be happening now but which will only become apparent at some point in the future:

I expect that he*'ll have been drinking* on the way home.
She got paid today, so perhaps she*'ll have been feeling* happier.

3.4 *Be going to*

> She*'s going to buy* herself a new coat.
> Look at those clouds. I think it*'s going to rain*.

■ Be going to + the base form has two different meanings:

– Future of present intention. The subject is nearly always a person and the sentence says what this person intends to do:

> We*'re going to have* a party.
> He*'s going to be* a priest when he grows up.
> I *am not going to tell* you again!

Compare

••

Compare the use of be going to to show intention with will to make a promise or offer:

> *Anne:* **Fred! That shelf is falling down.**
> *Fred:* **Don't worry. I'll mend it.** (= promise or offer)
> *Fred starts collecting the tools. Bill comes in.*
> *Bill:* **What are you doing?**
> *Fred:* **I'm going to mend the shelf.** (= intention)

••

– Future of present cause. Be going to indicates something that the speaker thinks will happen because its causes are already present. Such events are unlikely to be in the distant future:

> **'Mummy, why's that woman so fat?' 'She*'s going to have* a baby.'** NOT **'She will have a baby.'**
> **Have you heard the news? There*'s going to be* an election.**
> **Be careful! You*'re going to drop* those plates.**

■ Be going to is also used to express determination:

> I*'m going to tell* her what I think of her.

3.5 The present progressive with future meaning

> I*'m starting* a new job on Monday.
> We *are interviewing* applicants all next week.

The form of the present progressive – be + the -ing form of the verb – is discussed at **1.5**.

■ The present progressive is used to describe fixed arrangements and plans. The subject is usually a person. Since the arrangements have already been made, the event is unlikely to be in the distant future.

■ The present progressive usually describes events which are actually going on. To avoid confusion, when it has future meaning there is often a time expression like **soon, later, next week** or **in two months** to say exactly when the event will take place. The future use of the present progressive is very common with verbs indicating motion:

Steve*'s coming* **home tomorrow.**
They*'re arriving* **at one o'clock and** *leaving* **at three.**
'What *are you doing* **next week?' 'We***'re going* **to Norwich.'**
Sara*'s taking* **the 12.40 plane.**
Are you staying **in a hotel or with friends?**

3.6 The future progressive: *will/shall* + *be* + *-ing*

The Cardiff train *will be arriving* **on Platform 4.**
The sun *will be setting* **in ten minutes.**

■ Will/shall + be + the -ing form is used for planned or predictable events in the near but not immediate future. It should be compared with the future using will/shall + base form: will/shall alone often suggests ideas of promising, offering or requesting; will/shall + be + the -ing form lacks these connotations, and is therefore used when they are inappropriate or when the speaker deliberately wants to avoid them.

Will/shall + be + the -ing form can thus be summed up as the 'future which will happen anyway':

Will Denise come **to your party?** (= Has Denise agreed to come to your party?)
Will Denise be coming **to your party?** (= Do you know whether Denise is intending to be at your party?)

■ The future progressive is used to talk about an event which covers a limited period and which will be in progress at a specified moment in the future:

At 6 o'clock I*'ll be driving* **home from work.**
She*'ll* **probably** *be watching* **television when we call.**

■ The future progressive is used for politeness when asking about somebody's plans. Compare the following pairs of sentences:

Will you sing **for us?** (= Please sing for us.)
Will you be singing **for us?** (= Do you plan to sing for us anyway?)

I'll cook **dinner this evening if you're too tired.**
I'll be cooking **dinner this evening – it's my turn.**

3.7 The simple present with future meaning

The plane *leaves* **in ten minutes.**
Does **the match** *start* **at three or three thirty?**

For the form of the simple present, see **1.1**.

■ The simple present is used for the future in three main ways:

– In clauses beginning with if, when, etc:

If he *phones* **this evening, tell him I'll call him back.**
The town will be much quieter after the tourists *leave.*

– When the event described is an unalterable fact:

Christmas Day *falls* on a Wednesday this year.
The sun *rises* at 7.15 tomorrow morning.

– When the speaker thinks of the event as having been decided or arranged so certainly that it cannot be changed. It is especially common for describing journeys planned for the near future and timetables:

Autumn term *starts* on 8 September.
When I *die*, my money *goes* to my children.
We *start* from London and *spend* the first night in Maldon.
Then we *go* on to Ipswich.

3.8 *Be to* + the base form of the verb

■ Be to + the base form of the verb is used to give the idea of a duty or plan that someone else has arranged for the subject. Its meaning is close to that of 'be supposed to':

We*'re to meet* outside the station at 10 o'clock.

■ In questions it often has a tone of shock or disbelief:

Am I *to believe* a story like that?

3.9 *Be about to* + the base form of the verb

■ Be about to is used to describe events which will happen in the very near future:

The train*'s about to leave*.
He seemed *to be about to say* something before he died.

3.10 The future in the past

The past tense forms of will/shall, be going to and will/shall + be + the -ing form are used to indicate 'future in the past'; that is, they show that at some time in the past an event had yet to happen. The simple past is not used in this sense, and the past progressive only very rarely. In general, the difference in meaning between the various forms is parallel to that between their present tenses.

Would/should

You said that you *would pay* us within ten days.
I knew that he*'d arrive* on time – and here he is!
I hoped she *wouldn't be* angry.
They forgot to tell us when the wedding *would be*.

■ Would/should is used as the past tense of will/shall mainly in that clauses and other noun clauses (⇨ **SYNTAX 2, 6.**). The difference between would and should is the same as that between will and shall (⇨ **3.1**). Should is rare with a future-in-the-past sense.

■ For the contracted forms of would and should, see **VERBS 1, 2.7**.

■ For other uses of would and should, see VERBS **1, 3.5 & 3.6**.

Was/were going to

> **They *were going to visit* you but they had to work late.**
> **She *was going to study* medicine but she failed the examination.**
> **I thought you *were going to be* sick.**
> **The sky was black and it seemed that it *was going to rain*.**

■ The past forms of be going to are the commonest way of indicating future in the past in main clauses. They are also used in other clauses.

Would/should + be + the -ing form

> **The driver said that the bus *would be leaving* in ten minutes.**
> **She asked me if I'*d be working* late.**

■ Like would/should, would/should + be + the -ing form is used primarily in that clauses and other noun clauses. It is the natural choice for a past-tense version of the present progressive with future meaning:

> **Brian said that he *would be playing* football this afternoon.**

Verbs 3

1. The Imperative
Shut up and sit down!

2. The Subjunctive
I suggest you be quiet.

3. The Passive
I was told to be quiet.

4. The *to* Infinitive
It was rude to shout like that.

5. The *-ing* Form
Shouting is unnecessary.

6. The Past Participle
Afraid of another argument, he kept quiet.

1. The Imperative

> **Shut up! Go away! Get lost!**
> **Please remember to post my letter.**
> **Don't do anything stupid. Don't be rude!**
> **Be good! Always be kind to animals.**

■ The imperative is used to give orders or to make an offer or an invitation. The form is the same in both the singular and plural.

– Positive commands: base form of the verb (without subject)

– Negative commands: **don't** + the base form (without subject)

The imperative of the verb **be** is simply **be**.

■ Especially in polite commands, such as offers and invitations, the positive auxiliary **do** is sometimes used:
> ***Do* have another piece of cake.**

■ The imperative may have a subject, usually **you**, when the speaker wants to make it clear who they are talking to, or to add emphasis. In negative commands the subject goes after the **don't**:
> ***You* sit over there. *Everybody* be quiet.**
> **Don't *you* worry yourself about him.**

■ **Always** and **never** go before the imperative:
> ***Always* clean your teeth before going to bed.**
> ***Never* do that again.**

■ The imperative, even with **please**, is often considered impolite except when making offers or invitations. More polite commands

can be made using question forms of **can/could** and will/would:
> *Can* **you pass me the sugar, please?**

■ For extra politeness, the past tense forms **could** and **would** are used:
> *Could* **you give me a hand with this suitcase?**
> *Would* **you be so kind as to hold the door open for me?**

■ To make suggestions in which the speaker includes himself, the auxiliary **let's** (**not**) is added. The form is always contracted:
> *Let's go* **to the cinema this evening.**
> *Let's not think* **about it.**

■ Let is also used in commands directed to people other than 'you':
> **I don't care if he's in a hurry.** *Let him wait!*

■ The question form using **shall we** can be used to make suggestions equivalent to the **let's** construction:
> *Shall we* **take a drive in the country on Saturday?**

Another alternative is the expression What about + the -ing form:
> *What about getting* **a pizza?**

2. The Subjunctive

2.1 The present subjunctive

It is essential that he *do* the work properly.
They insisted that I not *be* told the truth.

Form

■ The present subjunctive uses the base form of the verb even in the third person singular. The present subjunctive of be is be. The negative is very rare; it is made by placing not before the verb.

Usage

■ The present subjunctive occurs in that clauses after verbs like ask, demand, insist, require, suggest, propose:

The prime minister suggested that he *resign.*

■ The present subjunctive is used after the construction it is important/necessary/essential that…:

It is essential she *speak* to me first.
It's very important he *pay* on time.

─ **Note** ─────────────────

The present subjunctive is found mainly in American English. British English prefers to use the auxiliary should (⇨ **VERBS 1, 3.6**) or other forms such as the to infinitive.

It's very important that they *should* be paid on time.
It's very important for them *to be paid* on time.

2.2 The past subjunctive

I wouldn't do that if I *were* you.
He shouted and jumped about as if he *were* mad.

Form

■ The past subjunctive of be is were even in the first and third persons singular. Otherwise the form is the same as the simple past (⇨ **VERBS 2, 2.1**).

Usage

■ This special use of were is found only in certain imaginary clauses such as if clauses (⇨ **SYNTAX 2, 4.**); clauses of comparison after as if and as though; and after verbs like wish. It is considered rather formal; informal English uses the simple past was:

I wish I *were/was* a little bit taller.

3. The Passive

Our school *was opened* by the Queen.
Have all the lights *been switched off?*

3.1 Form

■ The passive is made with the auxiliary be + the past participle. It is found in all tenses, both simple and compound, although the sequence **been being** is usually avoided. For the order of auxiliaries in compound tenses, see **Verbs 1, 2.8**.

Simple present	**Stamps *are sold* here.**
Present progressive	**My car *is being resprayed*.**
Simple past	**He *was arrested* yesterday.**
Past progressive	**The house *was being rebuilt*.**
Present perfect	**You *have been warned*!**
Past perfect	**I thought you *hade been told*.**
Future	**You *will be given* the keys tomorrow.**
Future perfect	**It *will have been moved* by then.**

■ The agent (the person or thing which brought about the action) is introduced by **by**. The instrument (what was used to make the action happen) is introduced by **with**:

The costumes were made *by* the children's mothers.
I was hurt *by* what he said.
He was killed *with* a knife.

■ Almost all verbs that can take an object can be made passive, including most phrasal verbs (➪ **Verbs 1, 4.1**) and Verb + Object + Verb constructions (➪ **Verbs 1, 5.2**):

The meeting *has been put off.*
You *were seen taking* money from the cash box.
The matter *will be dealt with* tomorrow.

■ Verbs which can have two objects have two different passives:

Simon gave Mandy a book. →
1. Mandy *was given* a book (by Simon).
2. The book *was given* to Mandy (by Simon).

Other common verbs which have two objects include: buy, lend, offer, pay, promise, refuse, send, show, tell, teach.

3.2 Usage

■ The passive is used when the speaker wants to emphasize the object of what would be the normal active sentence.

Active: **You can buy newspapers at the station.**
Passive: **Newspapers *can be bought* at the station.**

■ The passive is used frequently in particular kinds of English, especially business and technical English:

English *is spoken* here.

The printer *can be used* with most computers.

■ When the source of some information is not known or is considered to be unimportant, the construction it + passive is used:

***It's said* that prices are going up.**

***It is* widely *believed* that he was murdered.**

> ## Note
>
> Some verbs are used almost exclusively in the passive. These include: to be born, to be drowned.

3.3 The *get* passive

■ The be passive is often ambiguous – it can describe either a state or an event:

The window *was broken* all last winter.

The window *was broken* last night (by some kids throwing stones).

They *were married* for twenty-five years.

They *were married* at St Stephen's Church last Saturday.

■ In informal English, get is now more usual than be as a passive auxiliary when the sentence describes an event rather than a state:

The window *got broken* last night (by some kids throwing stones).

They *got married* at St Stephen's Church last Saturday.

■ In negative and question forms, get acts like a main verb:

He doesn't *get paid* as well as he should.

Did you *get* well *looked after?*

■ The get passive is often used to describe what someone does to himself/herself:

He *got* washed. (by himself)

He *was* washed. (by somebody else)

The get passive can also suggest that something happens unexpectedly or without preparation:

He *was* left behind. (on purpose)

He *got* left behind. (by accident)

> ## Note
>
> The get passive is very common in all types of English. However some people still dislike it and it is avoided in formal contexts.

3.4 The *have* passive

■ The have or *causative* passive is used to show that the subject causes someone to perform the action mentioned.

The construction is:

> *subject + have + direct object + past participle*

The neighbours *had* **him** *arrested*. (by the police)
She *is having* **the house** *painted*. (by someone else)

Compare

••

She has cut her hair. (she has done it herself)
She has had her hair cut. (by someone else)

••

4. The *to* Infinitive

> *To start* the motor, turn the key in the ignition.
> I'd prefer not *to have* been there.

4.1 Forms

■ The simple infinitive is made with to + the base form. In addition, there are progressive, perfect and passive forms. Their meanings are predictable from the usual meanings of the progressive (⇨ **VERBS 2, 1.4**), perfect (⇨ **VERBS 2, 2.7**), and passive (⇨ **3.**):

Simple infinitive – to write:
> **I'm trying *to write* a letter.**

Progressive infinitive – to be writing:
> **I'd like *to be writing* about something different.**

Perfect infinitive – to have written:
> **I need *to have written* three more essays by next week.**

Passive infinitive – to be written:
> **The sign needs *to be written* clearly.**

■ There are also more complex combinations. (For the order of the auxiliaries, see **VERBS 1, 2.8**):
> **This essay seems *to have been written* in a hurry.**
> **You seem *to have been writing* a lot of essays recently.**

■ The negative is formed by placing not before the to:
> **I'll try *not to think* about it.**
> **It's impossible *not to have been* impressed.**

■ The to infinitive does not usually need a subject. When a subject is required, it is preceded by for and put in the object case:
> **It will take a lot of time *for me to forget* her.**
> **There's no reason *for him to have said* that.**

4.2 Uses

The to infinitive is used in several different ways:

■ To express purpose:
> **I only said that *to shut him up*.**
> ***To do well*, you will need to work harder.**

The to is often strengthened as in order to or so as to:
> **They went to France *in order to see* their cousins.**

In negative sentences, to is usually replaced by in order not to or so as not to:
> **We were very quiet, *so as not to* annoy her any more.**

■ As the subject of a sentence:
> ***To make* a few mistakes is quite understandable.**
> ***Not to buy* one now would be stupid.**

In normal usage, however, the infinitive is generally moved to the end of the clause and replaced by it (⇨ SYNTAX **1**, **2.2**):

> It's quite understandable *to make* a few mistakes.
> It was wrong of you *to lie* to me.
> Do you think it's a good idea for me *to speak* to him?

■ As the complement of some verbs (⇨ VERBS **1**, **5.1**), adjectives, and nouns:

> I want *to take* a bath.
> They're sure *to have* heard about it.
> He was happy for me *to know* the truth.
> There's no reason for you *to get* upset.
> He has a tendency *to tell* lies.

Note

American and British usage often differs, American preferring the to infinitive where British uses a preposition + -ing form (⇨ **5.**):
American:
> We have the possibility *to go out* tonight.

British:
> We've got the possibility *of going out* tonight.

■ After question words in reported questions and commands:

> They asked me *when to come/what to do.*
> They told me *where to go/who to speak to.*

■ After indefinite pronouns and similarly formed adverbs (⇨ PRONOUNS AND DETERMINERS, **7.**):

> Is there *anything to eat* in the house?
> My personal life is *nothing to do* with you.
> I'm looking for *somewhere to live.*

■ After too + an adjective or adverb; after adjectives or adverbs + enough; and after some comparatives:

> I'm afraid that it's *too late for you to see* him.
> You're not *old enough to see* this film.
> Do you think it's *better not to go?*

■ After certain fixed expressions such as:

> We've had *no time to* make dinner.
> There's *plenty of room* for you *to* make yourself comfortable.
> It's *not my job to* do the cleaning.
> Would you be *so kind as to* give me a hand with this?

5. The *-ing* Form

The thief broke in without *starting* the burglar alarm.
Not *having* read the book, I don't want to comment on it.

5.1 Forms

■ For the spelling of the -ing form, see **VERBS 1, 1.3**. Perfect and passive -ing forms are made using the -ing forms of the auxiliaries have and be:

Perfect – having written:
Excuse me for not *having written*.

Passive – being written:
I couldn't read it, on account of it *being written* so badly.

Perfect passive – having been written:
I'm very sorry about it *having been written* so badly.

■ The negative is made by placing not before the -ing form:
Not *having* a job isn't much fun.

■ When the -ing form has a different subject from the verb, an object pronoun is used:
I can't say anything without *him* criticizing me.

■ At the beginning of sentences the subject of an -ing form is usually in the possessive case. In formal English this is also true in other positions (⇨ **VERBS 1, 5.2**):
Their *knowing* him really surprised me.
I can't say anything without Harry's *criticizing* me.

5.2 Uses

The -ing form is used in several different ways:

■ As a noun, e.g. cooking (= the food someone cooks), teaching (= the profession of a teacher). These words are used like any other noun:
I love Chinese *cooking*.
We heard some *singing* from the other room.

■ As an adjective, e.g. boring, exciting, frightening. The -ing form of most verbs can be used adjectivally and is generally active in meaning (⇨ **ADJECTIVES, 1.5**):
They saw a *shining* light in the distance.
I find his absence rather *worrying*.

■ As a preposition, e.g. concerning, regarding, (not) counting:
I've had a letter *concerning* my tax payments.
There were four of us, *not counting* the dog.

■ To form progressive tenses (⇨ **VERBS 2, 1.5**):
Someone's been *trying* to phone you all day.

In normal usage the -ing form is generally moved to the end of the clause and replaced by it (⇨ **Syntax 1, 2.2**):

It might produce results, *sending* a letter to the manager.
It's amazing, him *turning out* to be a spy.

This construction is especially common in certain fixed expressions, mainly negative, e.g. after it's no fun/good/use:

***It's no good you(r) making* such a fuss.**
Do you think *it's worthwhile asking* Bob?

■ As the complement of some verbs (⇨ **Verbs 1, 5.1**):

He seems to *enjoy watching* football at weekends.
I *dislike her always looking* so untidy.

■ After prepositions:

He caught malaria *from drinking* infected water.
We were delayed *because of* the bus not *arriving* on time.
What *about taking* a couple of days off work?

This usage is particularly common after those verbs, adjectives, and nouns which are usually followed by prepositions:

I *forgot about* posting the letter.
Are you *interested in* going to the zoo tomorrow?
My *reason for* coming was that I wanted to see you.

■ After no in instructions and commands:

No smoking. No parking.
I'll allow *no talking* in this classroom.

■ After certain nouns to explain their meaning:

I've had some problems *starting* the engine.
They've passed a law *banning* strikes.

■ As the main verb in certain types of (non-finite) clause:

1. Clauses describing nouns. There are two types:

– The first is like a relative clause (⇨ **Syntax 2, 2.**) with who is/was etc removed, and follows the noun described:

We saw a man in a grey coat *sitting* at the table in the corner.
The train now *arriving* on platform six is the eight fifteen to Bristol.

– The other is found at the beginning or end of a main clause and describes its subject:

Meanwhile the bishop went around the guests, *bidding* them welcome.
***Running* down the street, I tripped over a stone.**
***Taking* all things into consideration, I'm going to buy that one.**

2. Clauses acting as a noun:

***Playing football* is my hobby.**
I don't like you *talking like that*.

3. Clauses acting adverbially, often after time conjunctions such as

when, while, before, since, and though:

> They were caught *while trying* to rob a bank.
> *After having* completed his degree, he went to work in London.
> *Though sharing* your doubts, I'm willing to give her the job.

Another type uses with + object pronoun + -ing form, and describes the general conditions of the main event:

> The company should do even better *with her now working* for us.
> *With tears rolling down* her face, she told me what had happened.

The with is usually omitted before being and perfect -ing forms:

> The weather *being* good, we decided to go for a walk.
> The children *having left home*, she decided to move to a smaller house.

6. The Past Participle

John stared out of the window, *lost* in thought.
The work will not be *paid* for unless *completed* on time.

6.1 Forms

■ For the past participle of regular and irregular verbs, see **Verbs 1, 1.6**.

■ The negative is made by placing not before the past participle:
This is a subject not *dealt* with in this book.

■ Except in perfect tenses, the past participle always has a passive meaning.

6.2 Uses

The past participle is used in several different ways:

■ As an adjective, e.g. bored, tired, well-known. The past participle of most verbs can be used adjectivally and is generally passive in meaning (⇨ **Adjectives, 1.5**):
I cut myself on some *broken* glass.
She looks utterly *disgusted*.

■ To form the perfect tenses (⇨ **Verbs 2, 2.6**):
Who's *eaten* my sandwiches?

■ To form the passive (⇨ **Verbs 3, 3.**):
The train has *been delayed* by leaves on the line.
I hope you didn't *get lost*.

■ In certain Verb + Object + Verb constructions, all with a passive sense (⇨ **Verbs 1, 5.2**):
They want the parcel *delivered* immediately.
I had my kitchen *redecorated*.
She saw him *run over*.

■ As the main verb in certain types of (non-finite) clause. These constructions closely parallel those for the -ing form.

1. Clauses describing nouns. There are two types:

– The first is like a relative clause (⇨ **Syntax 2, 2.**) with who is/was etc removed, and follows the noun described:
We travelled through country *devastated* by war and famine.
Those *considered* responsible for the mistake were dismissed.

– The other is found at the beginning or end of a main clause and describes its subject:
***Taken* completely by surprise, I didn't know what to say.**
***Taken* as a whole, this plan has much to recommend it.**
The king addressed the ambassadors, *seated* on a golden throne.

2. Clauses acting adverbially, in particular after:

– conjunctions such as when, while, if and though:

When *cooked* properly, sausages make a fine meal.
The parcel can be sent express if *required*.
Though badly *wounded*, he managed to crawl back to the camp.

– the preposition with + object + past participle. This type of clause normally describes the general conditions of the main event:

The garden would get more light *with that tree cut down*.
***With him banned from driving*, there was no choice but to walk.**

A similar construction without with is used to show the conditions before the main event, and typically gives the reasons for it:

The work *finished*, we all went home.
They stood in silence, their eyes *fixed* on the horizon.

Adverbs and Adverbials

1. Adverbials
2. Adverbs

Adverbials are used to express how, where, how often or to what extent something happens. Adverbials are often

Adverbs
He *suddenly* leaped out of his seat.
She walked home *slowly*, lost in thought.

But adverbials can also be:

Adverb phrases
I've never seen anyone move *so quickly*.
He closed the door *very quietly*.

Prepositional phrases
He left *by the back door*.
We won the game *without much difficulty*.

Noun phrases
I saw him again *last night*.
He'll be leaving for America *next week*.

1. Adverbials

1.1 Usage

■ Adverbials describe the main action of the phrase or sentence. They can modify:
– verbs:
   He spoke *forcefully and intelligently*.
– adjectives:
   It's an *extremely moving* poem.
– other adverbials:
   He played *particularly badly* towards the end of the match.
– sentences:
   ***Occasionally, he would leave his car at home and walk to work*.**

1.2 Types of adverbial

Adverbs and adverbials are often categorized according to their function:
– Adverbials of manner:
   She danced *quite beautifully*.

– Adverbials of time:

He'll be leaving for American *soon*.

– Adverbials of frequency:

I *seldom* see him these days.

– Sentence Adverbs:

***Personally*, I don't believe a word of it.**

– Quantifiers:

I don't know him *well enough* to ask him.

– Intensifiers:

This meat tastes *extremely* unpleasant.

– Focusing Adverbs:

There are *only* three people who know about it.

1.3 Position of adverbials

There is some freedom about the position of adverbials in sentences. The main tendencies are these:

■ Adverbials are not usually placed between a verb and its object or, with phrasal verbs, between the verb and its particle (⇨ **VERBS 1, 4.**):

You'll see your cousins *soon*.

John turned up *late*.

We're looking forward to the game on Saturday *very much*.

■ Adverbials of manner and time usually go towards the end of the sentence:

He told us the news *briefly* and *clearly*.

Before you start, you should read all the questions *thoroughly*.

■ Certain adverbials always go at the end of the sentence, such as too (= 'also'), as well, (not)...yet, and (not)...either:

Andy sent me some flowers *too*.

Have you seen the new exhibition *yet*?

■ Adverbials of time and sentence adverbs can also be placed at the beginning of the sentence. Sentence adverbs apply to the sentence as a whole rather than individual words in it: for example, to make connections, e.g. however, in addition; and to show how desirable or true the speaker thinks the event is, e.g. luckily, unfortunately; probably, certainly:

***Suddenly* it started pouring with rain.**

***Firstly*, you're late. *Secondly*, you haven't got the money.**

***Regrettably*, I won't be able to come.**

■ Adverbials of frequency (always, sometimes, often, never, usually, etc) and adverbials describing the general time of an event (still, already, then, by now, etc) are usually placed:

– Between subject and verb if the verb is a single word:

I *never* saw them again.

– After the first auxiliary if the verb has auxiliaries (⇨ **VERBS 1, 2.**):

He's *always* complaining about his bad back.

I would *never* have done it if you had ever told me not to.
– After simple tenses of the verb be:

Your hands are *still* dirty.

■ Focusing adverbials like only and even are often used like adverbs of frequency (see above):

He didn't hit anyone. He *only* swore a few times.
Not only has he cleared the table, he's *even* done the washing up.

■ Adverbials describing adjectives or other adverbials go in front of the word they apply to. Focusing adverbials can also be used in this way. Enough goes after the word it applies to:

That was a very nice walk and now I'm feeling *much better*.
She arrive at the dance *elegantly* dressed in a silk kimono.
I was able to finish *only* the first three questions.
I'm afraid you're not old *enough* to see this film.

▶ Note that negative adverbs and 'semi-negative' adverbs (hardly, rarely, only) at the beginning of a sentence cause inversion of the verb and subject (⇨ **SYNTAX 1, 3.**):

Never in my life have I been so insulted.
= I have never been so insulted in my life.
Hardly had he entered when the telephone rang.
Only years later did I understand exactly what he had meant.

2. Adverbs

2.1 Form of adverbs

Regular forms

■ Most adverbs, especially manner adverbs, are formed by adding the suffix -ly to the adjective:

    slow → **slowly**
    clear → **clearly**

■ There are some minor variations:

-y	→	-ily	**happily, tidily, speedily**
-le	→	-ly	**gently, nobly**
-ll	→	-lly	**fully, dully**
-ic	→	-ically	**drastically, historically** BUT **publicly**

Irregular forms

■ Some common adverbs share the same forms as their corresponding adjectives or determiners, e.g. fast, late, early, right, wrong, hard; much, enough, either:

    I got to work *late*.
    You didn't know about it *either*.

■ Participles are treated in the same way as adjectives:

    boringly . tiredly . repeatedly

> When past participles are turned into adverbs, the -e before the -d is sometimes pronounced, e.g. **deserved** [dɪˈzɜːvd] but **deservedly** [dɪˈzɜːvɪdlɪ].

▶ Note that many words ending in -ly are adjectives, e.g. friendly, silly, likely. Such words can only be turned into adverbs by making complete phrases such as **in a friendly way/manner**.

Compare

•••

Some -ly adverbs do not correspond to the adjectives without the suffix, e.g. late (= not early) v. lately (= recently). Compare:

    I hit him as *hard* as I could. (= with force)
    I *hardly* hit him. (= barely; hardly at all)

•••

2.2 Comparison of adverbs

Regular forms

■ The vast majority of adverbs form their comparatives and superlatives by adding the words **more** and **most** (compare **ADJECTIVES, 2.**):

He spoke *more angrily* than he had before.

■ Some common adverbs have comparison with -er and -est, e.g. soon, fast, hard, long, late, early, near, close. For spelling rules, see **ADJECTIVES, 2.2**.

The builders completed the job *sooner* than I'd expected.
Who arrived *the earliest?*

Irregular forms

adv	comparative	superlative
well	better	best
badly	worse	worst
much	more	most
little	less	least
far	farther/further	farthest/furthest

■ 'Downward' comparison and comparison of equality with adverbs is the same as with adjectives (↪ **ADJECTIVES, 2.4**):

We have started to look at this matter *less favourably*.
She doesn't cook *as well as* her sister.

▶ Note that the comparative and superlative forms of adjectives are often used adverbially. In most cases this is optional:

Can't you work *a little quicker/more quickly?*

Prepositions

A preposition is one of a group of words used to express relationships (of time, manner, location, etc) between other words. They are used extensively in English and often prove problematic for learners.

1.1 Forms

■ Prepositions take one of two forms:
– single words: **at, between, in, on, up**
– two or more words: **apart from, in front of, instead of**
Some present participles are also used as prepositions:
   considering, following, leaving aside, regarding

1.2 Positions

■ Prepositions are found before:
– nouns and noun phrases:
   He went *up the stairs.*
   She sat *on the chair by the window.*
– the object form of pronouns (⇨ **PRONOUNS AND DETERMINERS, 1.**):
   A tall man stood *in front of her.*
   According to them, she'll easily win.
– wh- clauses:
   The man *to whom* she was speaking. *(formal)*
– -ing clauses/gerunds:
   Why don't you help *instead of just standing there.*
   He's worried *about falling.*

■ Prepositions are found after:
– verbs (⇨ **VERBS 1, 4. & 5.**):
   He *asked for* some more coffee.
   I've *thought about* this very carefully.
– adjectives (⇨ **ADJECTIVES**):
   I'm very *fond of* them.
   New York is *famous for* its skyline.
– nouns:
   He takes an *interest in* their studies.
   There was a *lack of* support for the proposal.

■ Prepositions are found at the end of a clause or sentence in:
– wh- questions (⇨ **PRONOUNS AND DETERMINERS, 9.1**):
   Who were you speaking *to?*
   What is this all *about?*
– relative clauses (⇨ **SYNTAX 2, 2.**):
   The group I went on holiday *with.*
– exclamations:
   What a state you're *in!*

– passives (⇨ **Verbs 3, 3.**):
  The matter has not yet been dealt *with*.
  Why is he crying? He's just been shouted *at*.
– infinitive clauses:
  It's a strong position to be *in*.

▶Note that prepositions are *not* found before:

– that clauses:
  He relied on her being efficient.
  NOT **He relied on that she was efficient.**
– the *to* infinitive (⇨ **Verbs 3, 4.**):
  He left early to catch the last bus.
  NOT **He left early for to catch the last bus.**
– the subject form of personal pronouns (⇨ **Pronouns and Determiners, 1.**):
  He moved towards me. *NOT* **He moved towards I.**

1.3 Preposition or adverb?

■ Some prepositions can also function as adverbs or adverbial particles. All prepositions must be followed by an object. If no object is present, the word is an adverb:
  The car rolled *down* the hill. (preposition)
  The car broke *down*. (adverb)

For more details on phrasal and prepositional verbs see **Verbs 1, 4.**

1.4 Meanings

■ Many prepositions have several different meanings which must be learned individually. Some meanings can be identified, however, according to the relationships formed between words:

– direction: from, into, off, to, towards:
  He dashed *from* the bathroom *into* the bedroom.
– location: above, at, behind, in, in front of, inside, next to:
  It's *behind* the cinema, *next to* the bank.
– manner: by, in, on, with:
  by car ⸳ *in* a loud voice ⸳ *on* foot ⸳ *with* a laugh
– a precise point in time: at, in, on:
  at five o'clock ⸳ *in* May ⸳ *on* Saturday
– a period of time: after, before, from, since, until:
  I went to Paris *for* three weeks/*during* the holidays.

▶ Note the difference between for and during:
For answers the question 'How long?'
During answers the question 'When?'

Throughout emphasizes that an action or event lasts from the beginning to the end of a period of time:
  He was in France *throughout* the war. (from start to finish)
  He was in France *during* the war. (at some point during the war)

Syntax 1

1. **Basic Word Order**
2. **Other Statement Patterns**
3. **Negative Sentences**
4. **Questions and Answers**
5. **Exclamatory Sentences**

1. Basic Word Order

1.1 Clause constituents

■ Clauses in English are made up of the following seven constituents:

Subject – S
All clauses need a subject, except imperatives (⇨ **VERBS 3, 1.**). The subject usually goes directly before the verb. The commonest types of subject are nouns or pronouns; when they are personal pronouns the subject form is used (⇨ **PRONOUNS AND DETERMINERS, 1.1**):

> *My father* works with your mother.
> *He* works with your mother.

Noun clauses (⇨ **SYNTAX 2, 6.**) and -ing forms (⇨ **VERBS 1, 1.3**) can also act as subjects:

> *What you said* was untrue.
> *Learning English well* takes a lot of time.

Verb – V
The verb can be a single word or group of words including a main verb and one or more auxiliaries (⇨ **VERBS 1, 2. & 3.**).

Direct Object – Od
Direct objects are normally nouns, pronouns or noun phrases but can be whole clauses. Direct objects typically go after the verb. They can have the same forms as subjects. When they are personal pronouns the object form is used (⇨ **PRONOUNS AND DETERMINERS, 1.1**):

> I saw *Rebecca* yesterday.
> I saw *her* yesterday.
> Danny said that *he was going.*
> I don't enjoy *working so hard.*

Direct objects can become the subject of passive sentences (⇨ **VERBS 3, 3.**):

I shot *the sheriff.* → *The sheriff* was shot.

Indirect Object – Oi
Indirect objects can only be nouns or pronouns; when they are personal pronouns the object form is used (⇨ **Pronouns and Determiners, 1.1**):

The artist showed *Cheryl* his paintings.
The artist showed *her* his paintings.

Indirect objects can become the subject of passive sentences (⇨ **Verbs 3, 3.**):

***She* was shown his paintings.**

Subject Complement – Cs
Verbs of 'being' or 'becoming' (e.g. be, seem, smell, look) are followed by subject complements – either adjectives or nouns:

The food smells *good*.
Tessa became *an actress*.

Object Complement – Co
Object complements follow the direct object of certain verbs. They are either adjectives or nouns:

The company made him *successful/a manager*.

Adverbial — A
Adverbials can be adverbs, prepositional phrases, adverb clauses, and other things. They show when, where, how, etc. the event took place. They are usually optional and can appear in various places in the clause (⇨ **Adverbs and Adverbials, 1.**):

***Last night* we went out with some friends to the theatre.**

1.2 Clause patterns

To a large extent the verb decides the constituents in a clause. There are seven patterns:

S + V
■ Verbs in such constructions are normally intransitive, e.g. come, go, sit, wait, work, and phrasal verbs like take off, slow down, sit down:

They're coming.
I gave up.

■ Sentences of only two words are unusual in English. Usually, to avoid sounding unnatural, the meaning of most sentences must be completed either by a direct object or an adverbial:

I work *(in a bank/very hard/on Friday night)*.

S + V + O
■ The verb here is normally a transitive verb, e.g. use, like, want, bring, enjoy:

Ruth uses a horrible perfume.

Many phrasal verbs and all prepositional verbs are transitive (⇨ **Verbs 1, 4.**):

> **Please turn on the radio.**
> **I looked carefully at the drawings.**

■ Very few verbs need a direct object. Far more common are verbs which can have an object, but can also be without one.

■ Other verbs are usually intransitive but can have certain kinds of objects in special circumstances:

> **Can you dance the tango?**

Sometimes the choice is completely open:

> **I read a good novel last night – I was reading all last night.**

Sometimes the two uses have rather different meanings:

> **Arthur drinks milk.**
> **Arthur drinks.** (i.e. too much alcohol)

S + V + Oi + Od

■ Some verbs can have two objects, e.g. give, send, tell, make, cook:

> **They've sent me another letter.**
> **Bert baked his wife a birthday cake.**

■ The indirect object ('person object') always goes before the direct object ('thing object'). With the single exception of **hand**, no verb has to have an indirect object:

> **They posted (her) the letter.**
> **They handed her the letter.**

■ With the single exception of **tell**, if there is an indirect object there must also be a direct object:

> **Chris told me.**
> **Chris told a story.**
> **Chris told me a story.**

■ There are two main types of verbs that can have indirect objects:

– Verbs of giving or transmitting: e.g. give, send, throw, offer, show, pay, teach. The indirect objects of these verbs can be replaced by a phrase beginning with **to**:

> **Mick threw me the ball.** → **Mick threw the ball to me.**

– Verbs of creating or helping: e.g. make, do, build, find, sing. The indirect objects of these verbs can be replaced by a phrase beginning with **for**:

> **Mick found me my hat.** → **Mick found my hat for me.**

■ The indirect objects of certain verbs, e.g. bet, save, cannot be replaced by a phrase:

> **They bet me £10 that I wouldn't win.**
> **Your help saved me a lot of time.**

■ The indirect object is replaced by a phrase:

a. When the direct object is short and the indirect object long:
   I gave it to *the woman in the red coat.*

b. In passive sentences:
   The parcel was sent *to the head office.*

c. In questions:
   Who* did you knit that pullover *for?

d. In relative clauses:
   That's *the man who I paid the money to.*

S + V + A
A few verbs cannot be used without an adverbial:
   My grandparents live in Liverpool.
   The show will last for ninety minutes.

S + V + Od + A
A few verbs require an adverbial of place after the direct object, e.g. put, set, place, stick, shove:
   I put the book on the shelf.
   She drove me to London.

The adverbial is generally optional. Some verbs allow two different S+V+Od+A patterns:
   The car splashed me with mud. = The car splashed mud over me.

S + V + Cs

■ Two types of verbs take subject complements:

– Verbs of being, e.g. be, look, appear, seem, taste:
   The tree is in the garden.
   The food smells wonderful.

– Verbs of becoming, e.g. become, get, turn:
   Later she became a famous film-star.
   The weather has turned cold.

■ Some verbs (such as get and turn) allow only adjective complements. Be also takes prepositional phrases, adverbs and clauses as complements:
   Lisa seems very rich/a very rich woman.
   Alan is getting fat. *BUT NOT* **Alan is getting a very fat man.**
   The plate is on the table.
   My excuse is that I forgot.

S + V + Od + Co

■ Object complements describe the object rather than the subject. Some verbs have only noun object complements, e.g. **appoint**, **choose**; others have only adjectives, e.g. **drive**, **get**; others allow both types, e.g. **make**, **consider**:
   The army proclaimed Caesar their leader.
   That noise is driving me crazy.
   You've made me very happy/a very happy man.

1.3 Verbs with multiple complementation patterns

Many verbs use various different patterns, depending on the meaning. For example get:

S+V+O: **Judy got a present.**

S+V+Oi+Od: **Tina got Judy a present.**

S+V+A: **They got home late.**

S+V+Od+A: **I got the parcel to the post office on time.**

S+V+Cs: **She got more and more tired.**

S+V+Od+Cs: **He got me really angry.**

1.4 Note on the verb *be*

The verb be is used in English as a main verb in some ways that foreign learners often find strange. In most cases get can be used in the same ways if the state described is starting rather than just existing:

1. Describing people's bodily sensations and attitudes, e.g. hot, sleepy, right, afraid, lucky:
   Are **you afraid of spiders?**
   I *am* **right and you are wrong.**
   There was no heating and we all *got* **very cold.**

2. Describing the weather:
   It's raining.
   It's getting too cold to go out.

3. What + be + like is used in questions to ask about the general nature of a person or event:
   I haven't met her. *What's she like?*
   What was it like **appearing on television?**

4. In expressions of distance:
   It's a long way from here to California.

2. Other Statement Patterns

English uses a number of other clause patterns, usually for clarity or to give special emphasis.

2.1 Existential sentences: *there* + *be*

> **There's a pie in the oven for your dinner.**
> **Will there be anyone I know at the party?**

■ This form is used to draw attention to the existence of something or to an event. The verb can be in any tense, and usually agrees in number with what comes after it. Sometimes, in informal and spoken English, a singular verb is used even if the noun is plural:

> *There's* **lots of things that we still need to discuss.**

■ The word there also appears in tag questions (⇨ **4.5**):

> *There hasn't* **been much rain recently, *has there?***

2.2 Extraposition

■ English tends to avoid sentences starting with subject that clauses, to infinitives (⇨ **Verbs 3, 4.**) or -ing forms (⇨ **Verbs 3, 5.**). In such cases the subject is usually moved to the end and replaced by it:

> **That he will come is certain.** → **It's certain that he will come.**
> **Would to go by bus be better?** → **Would it be better to go by bus?**
> **Thinking about it is painful.** → **It's painful thinking about it.**

Some verbs always use this kind of construction:

> **It seems that he won't be there.**
> **It occurred to me that I'd seen them before.**
> **It was reported that she had been killed.**

■ Similar types of object are sometimes treated in the same way:

> **I take it that you won't be coming.**
> **They kept it a secret that they were going to be married.**

2.3 Impersonal verbs

Verbs describing the weather follow the subject it and are always in the third person singular:

> **It's snowing again.**
> **It hasn't rained here for weeks.**
> **Thank goodness! It's clearing up at last.**

2.4 Cleft sentences

■ Cleft sentences are used to focus attention on a particular element or theme in a sentence which may or may not be the subject. The following examples show how the focus is changed by turning the sentence into a cleft sentence:

> **I enjoy myself most with you.** → **It's with *you* that I enjoy myself the most.**
> **Your letter originally gave me the idea.** → **It was *your letter* that originally gave me the idea.**

■ Cleft sentences have the general form:

> It + BE + *theme* + that (or occasionally who) + …

■ The verb is always singular and can be in any tense. Anything can be made the focus of a cleft sentence except complements (⟹ **1.1**) and, usually, verbs:

Subject:	**It was *John* that told me.**
Direct object:	**In the end it was *the Ford* that he bought.**
Indirect object:	**Was it *Bill* that you gave the money to?**
Adverbials:	**It was *at school* that I met him first.**
	It was *then* that I made my decision.

2.5 Thematic fronting

■ Another method of pointing out the theme of a sentence is to move it to the beginning and replace it in the main sentence with a pronoun. This is especially common when the sentence contains some element which is so long that it makes the sentence clumsy. Though common, thematic fronting is used less frequently in English than in other languages. It is also considered fairly informal:

> **That girl I saw you with yesterday, was she your sister?**
> **The computer I was going to buy, I'm afraid I've discovered that it's too expensive.**
> **Anyone who is interested, will they please let me know at once?**

■ Another kind of fronting occurs in situational sentences like:

> **Down we go!** ⹁ **Back came John.**

2.6 Special emphasis

> **I've met him ONCE, but I'd hardly say I knew him.**
> **You should EARN some money, not just borrow it.**

■ Individual items within sentences can be emphasized by intonation. This is common when the most important word in a sentence is not near the end. In the following examples the capitalized words would be stressed:

> **You should listen to ME, not to HIM.**
> **I said it was BESIDE the box, not IN it.**
> **The RED car is the one I was talking about.**

■ To give emphasis to a whole sentence – for instance, when disputing something someone else has said – the (first) auxiliary (or be) is stressed. In the simple present and past tenses, where there are no auxiliaries, the relevant form of do is inserted (⇨ **Verbs 1, 2.4**):

Don't believe him. I CAN play the violin.
There's no need to be angry. We HAVE done the washing up.
I'm not very fond of ice cream, but I DO like chocolate.
I DID remember to post your letter.

■ When the sentence is negative, the same effect can be made by using uncontracted forms and stressing the word not:

You must NOT leave the school at lunchtime.
I may have been a bit rude, but I did NOT swear.

3. Negative Sentences

3.1 Use of *not*

■ Most negative statements are formed using the word not, which goes after the first auxiliary or main verb be. In speech and informal writing people usually use the contracted form of the auxiliary + not (⇨ **Verbs 1, 2.7**):

He *will not* attend the dinner after all.
The bus *won't* have arrived by 8.30.
Our teacher *wasn't* very pleased with us.
If you *hadn't* told me I *wouldn't* have known.

■ But not is sometimes placed in front of the word it applies to:

The weather has been *not* bad.
We met the Joneses *not* in Italy but in Switzerland.
Not all her ideas are good.

■ The simple past and present tenses do not have auxiliaries. In such cases the relevant forms of auxiliary do are inserted (⇨ **Verbs 1, 2.4**).

Present tense

	Singular	Plural
1st person	I don't know	we don't know
2nd person	you don't know	you don't know
3rd person	he/she/it doesn't know	they don't know

Peter rides a bike. → Peter doesn't ride a bike.
The British drink coffee. → The British don't drink coffee.

Past tense. The form didn't is used throughout:

You remembered my birthday. → You didn't remember my birthday.
George drove to work today. → George didn't drive to work today.

3.2 Other negative words

■ English has a number of other negative words, e.g. never, nothing, no one, nowhere, as well as various expressions using the determiner no, e.g. in no way, on no account. Never, like not, is generally placed after the first auxiliary; the other negative words go:

– before the noun if they are determiners:

I have *never* been to Spain.
There are *no* biscuits left in the tin.

– before the verb if they are pronouns:

Nothing can stop me from winning.

■ A sentence containing a negative word can often be remade using not + a positive word. This is the normal usage; using the negative word alone is emphatic:

We haven't seen *anyone*. We've seen *no one*.

I didn't learn *anything*. I learnt *nothing*.

■ English also has a number of 'semi-negative' words, e.g. **hardly**, **scarcely**, and **only**. They usually go in front of the word they describe:

I *hardly* know him.
I've met her *only* three times = I've *only* met her three times.

■ In formal usage, negative adverbs and phrases, e.g. **never**, **on no account**, and semi-negative expressions, e.g. **hardly**, **only then**, can go at the beginning of a sentence. In such cases the (first) auxiliary is placed in front of the subject (➪ VERBS **1, 2.8**):

On no account should you tell him what we're planning.
Little did I know that he would return later.

3.3 Double negatives

■ In Standard English there is never more than one negative expression in a single clause:

You never tell me anything.
No one ever saw her again.

■ A minor exception occurs in sentences like:

We can hardly not tell them. → We really have to tell them.

■ In many non-standard dialects, however, double negatives are common:

I haven't done nothing wrong.

3.4 Transferred negation

■ When verbs like **think**, **believe**, **suppose**, **imagine** and **expect** are followed by a **that** clause with negative meaning, the **not** is usually 'transferred' to the main verb:

I think that he won't come. → I don't think that he'll come.
I suppose she doesn't know. → I don't suppose she knows.

The same occurs when these verbs are followed by a **to** infinitive (➪ VERBS **3, 4.**):

I expect not to see him. → I don't expect to see him.

Compare

• •

'Transferred negation' is only used with certain verbs. It is not, for instance, used with **say** and **tell**. The following sentences do not mean the same:

You didn't tell me to wash the car.
(= You didn't say anything about washing the car.)
You told me not to wash the car.
(= You said that I shouldn't wash the car.)

• •

3.5 Non-affirmative forms

> **I don't have any money.**
> **We haven't seen it yet.**

Certain determiners, pronouns and adverbs have special forms when used in negative and semi-negative sentences, called the 'non-affirmative' forms. They are also sometimes used in questions (➪ **4.**) and if clauses (➪ **Syntax 2, 4.**). The commonest of them are:

■ some, someone, something, etc → any, anyone, anything, etc (➪ **Pronouns and Determiners, 6. & 7.**):

> **You did some of things I told you to.**
> **You didn't do any of the things I told you to.**
> **Wayne said something.**
> **Wayne didn't say anything.**
> **I think I've seen it somewhere.**
> **I don't think I've seen it anywhere.**
> **Haven't you got any idea of the time?**
> **There's hardly anyone here.**
> **I'd have told you if I'd known anything about it.**

For special emphasis, not…any can often be replaced by no, none, no one, etc:

> **You did *none* of the things I told you to.**
> **Wayne said *nothing*.**

■ a lot of, lots of → much (+ uncountable noun), many (+ plural noun) (➪ **Pronouns and Determiners, 6.3**):

> **I haven't got *much* time.**
> **There weren't *many* people at school today.**
> **Do you see *much* of them these days?**

This is the normal usage. But a lot of and lots of can appear in negative sentences and questions; and much and many can appear in positive statements, particularly as subjects and after too and so:

> **There's not *a lot* to do here. = There isn't *much* to do here.**
> ***Much* of what you say is certainly true.**
> **I think I've eaten *too much*.**

Determiners and pronouns such as little, a little and few, a few (➪ **Pronouns and Determiners, 6.**) can also be viewed as changing to much and many:

> **I know *a few* people here. → I don't know *many* people here.**

■ already → yet. These adverbs are very common in sentences in the perfect tenses (➪ **Verbs 2, 2.6**). Yet is always placed at the end of its sentence:

> **My cousins have *already* arrived.**
> **→ My cousins haven't arrived *yet*.**
> **Have you finished your homework *yet*?**

■ still → any more, any longer

She's *still* complaining. → She isn't complaining *any more*.

■ too → either

I was there *too*. → I wasn't there *either*.
I hardly know them *either*.

■ too → enough

The pudding's *too* sweet. → The pudding's not sweet *enough*.

■ a long way → far; a long time → long

They've come *a long way*. → They haven't come *far*.
We stayed there *a long time*. → We didn't stay there *long*.

4. Questions and Answers

■ English has two main types of question:

1. yes/no questions, which expect the answer yes or no:
   'Can you swim?' 'Yes, I can.'/'No, I can't.'
   'Do you know German?' 'Yes, I do.'/'No, I don't.'/'Not much.'

2. WH- questions, which ask the listener to supply information. They contain words like who, what, when, where, why, or how (⇨ PRONOUNS AND DETERMINERS, 9.):
   'What is that instrument?' 'It's a clarinet.'
   'Who are you going to see?' 'Trevor.'/'No one special.'
   'When did they get back?' 'At 6 o'clock.'/'They haven't yet.'

Yes/no questions are typically pronounced differently from WH-questions. Yes/no questions usually end with a rising tone, and WH- questions with a falling tone, like ordinary statements.

■ Other types of questions include:
– Negative Questions (⇨ **4.4**):
   Aren't you coming?

– Tag Questions (⇨ **4.5**):
   You are coming, aren't you?

– Reported questions. See Reported Speech (⇨ SYNTAX **2, 7.**):
   'Are you ill, Sue?' said Greg. → Greg asked Sue if she was ill.
   'Where do you live?' I asked. → I asked them where they lived.

4.1 Yes/no questions

■ These are formed by placing the (first) auxiliary in front of the subject (⇨ VERBS **1, 2.8**):

AUX + S + V
   Was it raining hard?
   Would you like a drink?
   Have those customers been waiting long?
   Will your cousin and her new boyfriend be coming on Saturday?

Be acts as an auxiliary even if it is the main verb of the sentence (⇨ VERBS **1, 2.2**):
   Is it possible to mend it?
   Were you happy with the result?

■ In tenses which do not have auxiliaries – the simple present and simple past – do is used to supply the necessary auxiliaries. The forms are the same as those used in negative sentences (⇨ **Verbs 1, 2.4**):

You read the Times?
→ **Do you read the Times?**
Carol knows your brother?
→ **Does Carol know your brother?**
They got home safely?
→ **Did they get home safely?**

Answering yes/no questions

■ Yes/no questions can often be answered by simply 'yes' or 'no'. But very often a shortened sentence is added (⇨ **Verbs 1, 2.8**):

Yes, + PERSONAL PRONOUN + AUXILIARY
No, + PERSONAL PRONOUN + AUXILIARY + n't

'Does Sam work here?' *'Yes, he does.'/'No, he doesn't.'*
'Would you like a drink?' *'Yes, we would.'/'No, we wouldn't.'*
'Is it raining?' *'Yes, it is.'/'No, it isn't.'*

■ There in there is, there are, etc acts in the same way as the personal pronouns:

'Have there been any visitors?' *'No, there haven't.'*

▶ Note that positive contractions are not used in shortened answers unless the word which would naturally follow is included:

'Are you interested in cricket?' *'Yes, I am.'/'No, I'm not.'*

■ Other typical shortened answers include I think so/I don't think so; I hope so/I hope not; and I'm afraid so/I'm afraid not:

'Did Dickens write any plays?' *'I don't think so.'*
'Will you be coming?' *'I hope so.'/'I'm afraid not.'*

Non-affirmative forms in yes/no questions

Yes/no questions use the same 'non-affirmative' forms that are used in negative sentences (⇨ **3.**). For example:

Have you got *any* **sugar?**
Do you know *much* **about computers?**
Has the newspaper arrived *yet?*

However, the ordinary forms used in positive statements also appear in yes/no questions:

Have you got *some* **sugar?**
Do you know *a lot* **about computers?**
Has the newspaper *already* **arrived?**

The difference is in the attitude of the speaker. The non-affirmative forms are used if the question is neutral. But by using the ordinary forms the speaker suggests that he expects the answer to be 'yes':

Do you know many people here? (I ask because I do not know.)
Do you know lots of people here? (It seems to me that you do.)

4.2 Questions with *or*

> **Do you drive to work *or* do you take the train?**
> **Are you coming home on time *or* do you expect to be late?**

■ Questions with or are simply two yes/no questions joined together. Material that is shared by both questions can usually be omitted from the second:

> **Did they fax *the message* or (did they) send *it* by post?**

■ Questions with or are usually answered by confirming the part that is true. The examples above might be answered:

> **I take the train.**
> **I expect to be late.**
> **They sent it by post.**

If neither is true, the usual answer would start with the word neither rather than not:

> **Neither. I cycle.**
> **Neither. They sent it by courier.**

4.3 WH- questions

> **What are you doing?**
> **Who gave you those lovely flowers?**
> **When do they expect to see him?**

■ WH- questions ask for information rather than just 'yes' or 'no'. They usually start with a pronoun or determiner like who, whom, whose, which or what; or an adverb like when, where, why or how. Other WH- forms include compounds like how long and how often (⟿ PRONOUNS AND DETERMINERS, **9.**).

■ How much can be either a determiner before uncountable nouns or a pronoun standing for an uncountable noun such as money. How many is used in the same way with plural nouns such as people (⟿ NOUNS, **1.3**):

> *How much* **butter do you need?**
> *How much* **does it cost?**
> *How many* **brothers have you got?**
> *How many* **were there at the concert?**

■ How can be followed by adjective + be to ask about size and age. It is also used to ask about health:

> *How tall* **is the Eiffel Tower?**
> *How old* **is your dog?**
> *How are you* **today?**

How and What...like: differences

How is used to ask about:
- temporary states:
    How's work at the moment?
- people's health:
    How are you?

What...like is used to ask about:
- permanent states:
    What is your house like?
- the weather:

Compare:

What's the weather like in Italy at the moment?
How is Sue? She's not feeling very well.
What is Sue like? She's quite tall with long hair.

■ Most of the WH- words can have **-ever** added to them, e.g. whoever, why ever. These forms are used in questions expressing surprise:

Whoever **could that be phoning so late?**
Why ever **did you say that?**

■ WH- words are often used alone. For instance, **What?** is used to ask someone to repeat what they have said. (This is considered rather rude; it is more polite to say **Pardon?**)

'I'll do it.' 'When?'
'We've got visitors this evening.' 'Who?'

The grammar of WH- questions

■ The WH- word is usually the first word of the question. In formal English, however, it can come after a preposition; in everyday English the preposition is usually at the end (⇨ **PRONOUNS AND DETERMINERS, 9.**):

In which **country were you born?** = *Which* **country were you born** *in?*
From whom **did you buy it?** = *Who* **did you buy it** *from?*

■ When the WH- word is anything other than the subject of the question, the remaining word order is the same as for yes/no questions. Do and does are used in simple present tense questions and did in past tense questions (⇨ **4.1**):

When are the guests coming?
How long have you been working in Belfast?
Why does Judy dislike me so much?
Who did you tell about the wedding?

■ When the WH- word is the subject of the question, or part of the subject, normal word order is used:

Who told you about the wedding?

Whose car was damaged worst?
How many of the other children in the class agree with you?

Answering WH- *questions*
'Who are you?' 'Hugh Hatherway.'
'Who broke the window?' 'Me/I did.'
'Why didn't they come?' 'Because it was raining.'

WH- questions ask for information. The answer does not have to be
a full sentence; it is enough to use only the part which supplies the
information. This can often be a SUBJECT + AUXILIARY shortened
sentence, just as when answering yes/no questions (⇨ **4.1**).

4.4 Negative Questions

Won't Bernie tell you?
Don't you know her?
Wasn't Adrian pleased with his results?

■ Negative questions are yes/no questions using negative forms of
auxiliaries or the main verb be. The contracted forms, e.g. won't,
can't, are used even in quite formal English (⇨ **VERBS 1, 2.7**). The
uncontracted forms are rare (or regional):
Will Bernie not tell you?
Do you not know her?

■ Negative questions use the non-affirmative forms listed in **3.5**:
Can't you do *anything* properly?
Isn't the dinner ready *yet*?

The meaning of negative questions
■ Negative questions are used when the speaker suspects that the
answer is 'no' and is surprised, shocked or disappointed that this
should be the case:
'Don't you like music?' 'No, not very much.'
'Can't Phil cook?' 'He can a bit, but not very well.'
'Aren't you coming?' 'I'm afraid I can't.'
'Won't you tell me?' 'Yes, all right'/'Definitely not.'

■ They are also used to seek confirmation of something the speaker
thinks is true:
'Wasn't it cold in Iceland?' 'Yes, very cold.'/'No, it wasn't too
bad.'
'Aren't they the Smiths?' 'Yes, I think they are.'/ 'No, I don't
think so.'
'Don't the French drink beer?' 'Some of them do.'/ 'No, they
prefer wine.'

Answering negative questions
■ When answering negative questions, a simple 'yes' or 'no' is not
enough. Something must be added: either the (PRONOUN) SUBJECT +
AUXILIARY, as with yes/no questions; or some other phrase to show

precisely what is meant by 'yes' or 'no':

'Won't she come?' 'Yes, she will.'/'No, she won't.'

'Don't you like ice cream?' 'Of course I do.'/'No, not much.'

For more examples see **VERBS 1, 2.8**.

4.5 Tag questions

'You can come tonight, *can't you?*' 'Yes, I can.'/'No, I can't.'

'The police didn't find it, *did they?*' 'Yes, they did.'/'No, they didn't.'

■ Tag questions are used to ask for confirmation. They consist of the statement that is to be confirmed, followed by a shortened yes/no question made up of the appropriate personal pronoun subject and auxiliary (➪ **VERBS 1, 2.8**).

■ Tag questions are answered in the same way as negative questions: that is, a simple 'yes' or 'no' is not usually enough:

'Mary's working now, isn't she?'

'Yes, she is.'/'No, she isn't.'

■ If the verb in the statement is positive, the auxiliary in the tag question is negative, and the expected answer is 'yes':

'It's been a lovely day, hasn't it?' 'It certainly has.'

■ If the verb in the statement is negative or semi-negative (➪ **3.**), the auxiliary in the tag question is positive, and the expected answer is 'no':

'That's not right, is it?' 'No, it isn't.'

'We can hardly say that, can we?' 'No, I don't suppose we can.'/'I don't see why not.'

■ When the statement lacks an auxiliary, the relevant form of auxiliary do is used in the tag question and answer:

'Amy speaks French, doesn't she?' 'Yes, she does.'/'Not as far as I know.'

'The team played well, didn't they?' 'Yes, they did.'/'I don't think so.'

■ There in there is, there are, etc acts in the same way as the personal pronouns:

'There's something wrong, isn't there?' 'Yes, there is.'/'No, there isn't.'

■ The semi-modals are not usually used in tag questions (➪ **VERBS 1, 3.8**):

'They used to live in York, didn't they?' 'Yes, they did.'

▶ Note the irregular negative tag of the first person singular of the verb be:

I am on time, aren't I?

5. Exclamatory Sentences

What an unusual dress she's wearing!
How tall he is!
What a load of rubbish!

■ Exclamatory sentences focus on some element in a sentence which is the cause of surprise or disgust. This element is moved to the beginning of the sentence: if it is a noun (or noun phrase), **what** is placed in front of it; if it is an adjective or adverb, **how** is used. The rest of the sentence remains the same:

You've got some nice friends. → *What nice friends* **you've got!**
Peter is clever. → *How clever* **Peter is!**
It happened very quickly. → *How quickly* **it happened!**

When **what** precedes a singular countable noun the indefinite article a(n) is retained:

This is a beautiful house. → **What** *a* **beautiful house (this is)!**

▶Note that positive contractions of auxiliaries or **be** cannot be used unless the word which would naturally follow is kept (⇨ **VERBS 1, 2.8**).

■ When the meaning is obvious, all of the sentence except the **what** or **how** phrase can be omitted:

What a lovely day (it is)!
What utter nonsense (you're talking)!
How disgusting (you are)!

Exclamatory sentences of this sort are quite rare. Surprise is usually shown in other ways, such as by using tag questions (⇨ **4.5**) or words such as **so** or **really**:

He is tall, *isn't he!*
He's *so* **tall!**
He's *really* **tall!**

■ Surprise can also be shown by using **yes/no** question forms. This is very common in American English, where the word **ever** is often placed before an adjective or adverb being focused on:

Haven't you grown!
Would you believe it!
Are you (ever) stupid!

Syntax 2

1. Comment Clauses

> You haven't met my cousins, *I believe.*
> *I wonder,* could that have been the fire alarm?
> It's a good idea, *don't you agree?*
> *As you probably know,* Amanda's leaving us to get married.

■ Comment clauses are short clauses which speakers use to show their attitude to what they are saying. They usually stand outside the structure of the rest of the sentence.

■ Comment clauses vary greatly in form. They can have statement form (I believe, I think, etc) or question form (isn't that so?, etc). Other types include subordinate as clauses, to infinitives, -ing forms and past participles:

> Their new house, *my brother was telling me,* is very large.
> *What's more,* he didn't even thank us.
> *To sum up,* this project is unlikely to prove successful.
> *Strictly speaking,* there are some other possibilities.
> *Put briefly,* there's been a serious mistake.

Comments introduced by I think are more closely integrated into the sentence. I think appears at the beginning of the relative clause (➪ **2.**):

> That's the house which *I think* my sister wanted to buy.
> Angus is the one *I think* will get the job.

2. Relative Clauses

Relative clauses describe nouns and are linked to the main clause with relative pronouns (⇨ PRONOUNS AND DETERMINERS, 10.):

That's the man who runs the disco in town.
We're looking for someone we can rely on.
Everyone whose name begins with an A should turn up on Monday.

■ There are two main types of relative clause: defining or identifying relative clauses and non-defining or non-identifying relative clauses.

2.1 Defining relative clauses

■ These are necessary to define which particular person or thing the noun refers to:

That's *the book that I enjoyed the most*.
I prefer *students who work hard*.

2.2 Non-defining relative clauses

■ These merely give extra information about a person or thing which is already fully defined:

Our history teacher, *who is very old*, is retiring next week.
Do you know Iris, who used to work here?

Non-defining relative clauses are also used to give more information about the contents of a whole sentence:

She's just got engaged, which has made her family very happy.

■ Non-defining relative clauses are used merely to give extra information about a noun which has already been fully defined; for instance, only non-defining relative clauses can follow a proper name:

Roy Black, who plays for Arsenal, is the new England captain.
We stayed on Tiree, which is a little island off the west coast of Scotland.

Differences between defining and non-defining relative clauses

1. Non-defining relative clauses cannot be introduced by that; i.e. the usual relative pronouns are which (for things and to describe whole facts or sentences), who or whom (for people), and whose.
2. They are often preceded (and followed) by a short pause in speech or a comma in writing.
3. They must be introduced by a relative pronoun. In a defining relative clause, the relative pronoun can be left out if it is the object of the clause (⇨ PRONOUNS AND DETERMINERS, 10.3):

That's the book (that) I enjoyed the most. (that = object)

I prefer students who work hard. (who = subject)
Do you know Iris, who used to work here? (= non-defining)
The new record by Sting, which came out last week, is very good.
You've done the housework, which is very kind of you.
You've done the housework, for which I am very grateful.
It's from my uncle, who(m) you met last year in Swansea.
That's our vicar, who(m) I've always had a great respect for.
That's our vicar, for whom I've always had a great respect.
The little girl, whose face was very dirty, asked me for money.

Compare

••

For practical purposes, there is very often little real difference between defining and non-defining relative clauses. But compare the following examples:

She spoke to the boy who answered rudely.
= She spoke to the one of the boys who (had already) answered rudely.
She spoke to the boy, who answered rudely.
= She spoke to the boy (we already know which boy) and then he answered her rudely.
We've cut down the trees which were rotten.
= We've cut down only those trees which were rotten (and left the good ones standing).
We've cut down the trees, which were rotten.
= We've cut down all the trees. (This is because) they were all rotten.

••

3. Adverbial Clauses

■ Adverbial clauses act like adverbs within a sentence; that is, they say when, where, why, how, etc the event took place (➪ **ADVERBS AND ADVERBIALS, 1.2**):

> We'll be back *before you leave.*
> I like Dave *because he makes me laugh.*

Adverbial clauses are classified according to their meaning and the kinds of conjunction used to introduce them. They can go before or after the main clause and usually use the same sentence patterns as main clauses (➪ **SYNTAX 1, 1.2**). Amongst the commonest are:

Time clauses

■ These are introduced by time conjunctions such as when, while, after, before, since, as, as soon as, until, once, now (that):

> I was working hard *while* you were wasting time.
> Don't do anything *until* I tell you to.
> *Once* I've prepared the meat I can start on the vegetables.

■ Time conjunctions can also introduce other constructions such as verb + -ing form (➪ **VERBS 3, 5.**), verb + past participle (➪ **VERBS 3, 6.**), or a simple adjective (➪ **ADJECTIVES**):

> I read a book *while waiting.*
> *When angry,* he goes very red in the face.

▶ Certain time clauses require the use of particular tenses. Note the use of:
  – the simple past after since in sentences with the main verb in the present perfect (➪ **VERBS 2, 2.9**)
  – the simple present in clauses with future meaning (➪ **VERBS 2, 3.7**):

> Duncan hasn't been back to work *since he had* the accident.
> I've known her *since we were* at school.
> We won't know *until she comes.*

Place clauses

■ These are introduced by where or wherever:

> I put your letters *where* I always put them.
> You will find war *wherever* there is hunger and poverty.

Clauses of reason or cause

■ These are introduced by because, since, as, for, seeing that/as:

> I was late *because* I missed the bus.
> *As* it's Saturday, I think I'll go into town.

■ Cause can also be expressed using with + -ing form (➪ **VERBS 3, 5.**):

> I feel uncomfortable *with all those people staring* at me.

Sometimes with can be omitted:

Money being short, I don't think we can afford to go away this year.

Clauses of purpose

■ These are introduced by in order that and so that:

I came *in order that* I might see the paintings.

It is much commoner, however, to use to, in order to or so as to + the base form of the verb (⇨ **Verbs 3, 4.**):

We hurried *so as not to miss* the beginning of the film.
I went to the library *to get* a little peace and quiet.

■ To say that something was done so that something else should not happen, the commonest construction is to stop + object (+ from) + -ing form:

We filled up the hole *to stop the wind (from) getting in*.
Why don't you do something *to stop the baby crying?*

Clauses of result

■ These are introduced by so, so that or, more commonly so...that or such...that:

I've prepared the food, *so* everything's ready for the party.
The concert was *so long that* I fell asleep in the middle.
You're making *such a noise that* you'll wake the baby.

Clauses of manner

■ These are introduced by (exactly, just) as or like:

Do it *exactly as* I've shown you.
Judy talks *just like* her brother does.

▶ Note that using like as a conjunction is much more common in American English than in British English:

It's just like I said it was.

■ Manner can also be expressed by the construction with + noun group + -ing form or past participle:

She stood in the doorway *with her umbrella dripping* on the floor.
You'd look better *with your hair combed*.
Paul strolled through the park *with his hands in his pockets*.

The conjunction can be omitted, especially when the adverbial clause follows the main clause:

Colin arrived home, his clothes torn and tattered.
Jo danced all night, her face happy and full of joy.

Concession clauses

■ These are introduced by though, although, even if, even though, while, etc. They mean 'despite the fact that...':

The leaves still aren't open *although* it's already April.
Neil kept going *even though* he was tired.

While this is certainly true, I'm not sure that it's relevant.

■ It is also possible to use the construction though + -ing form/past participle/adjective:

Though now over seventy, he still runs five miles a day.
Though found guilty, he was immediately released.

Conditional clauses

■ These are introduced by if, unless, in case, provided (that), and some other conjunctions (⇨ **4.**):

Mark won't pass his exams *unless* he works a bit harder.
I've bought some sandwiches *in case* we get hungry.

■ When the condition does not affect what happens in the main clause, other conjunctions are used, for example whether...or or whatever:

We'll enjoy ourselves *whether* we win or not.
I won't believe you *whatever* you say.

■ In speech, conditions are often made using the imperative + and/or:

Say that again and I'll hit you. = I'll hit you if you say that again.
Move back or I'll shoot. = I'll shoot if you don't move back.

■ The constructions if, unless, etc + -ing form/past participle/ adjective etc are also possible:

He can get really unpleasant *if angered*.
We'll have a good time, *whatever the weather*.

4. *If* Sentences

If clauses are a special kind of adverbial clause (⇨ **3.**). English uses three types of if sentences, distinguished by meaning and the tense forms used in them:

1. Open or real conditions:

   If I pass my exams, my parents will be happy.

2. Remote conditions:

   If I passed my exams, my parents would be happy.

3. Hypothetical conditions:

   If I had passed my exams, my parents would have been happy.

Remote and hypothetical conditions have much in common and are sometimes together called *imaginary conditions.*

4.1 Non-affirmative forms

■ If clauses tend to use the non-affirmative forms of pronouns and determiners like any (for some) and much (for a lot of) (⇨ **Syntax 1, 3.5**). The usage is the same as in questions (⇨ **Syntax 1, 4.1**): the non-affirmative forms are the norm but the ordinary forms are used if the speaker feels that the thing should or might exist:

   If I had *any* money (at all), I'd lend you some.
   If I had *some* more money, I could buy another CD.

■ The non-affirmative adverb forms like yet (for already) and either (for too) are not usually used in if clauses:

   If Arthur's *already* here, send him up.

4.2 Open conditions

■ Open conditions are 'neutral' as to whether the if clause is true or not.

■ When the sentence refers to something in the future (as it often does), the verb in the if clause is in the present tense (⇨ **Verbs 2, 3.7**):

   If you *say* that again I'll get very angry.
   We'll go to the zoo tomorrow if it *doesn't* rain.

■ Other tense combinations are also possible, depending on meaning:

   We always have a good time if Charlie comes.
   If you haven't seen this film, go and see it now.
   If the programme started at eight, it should be over by now.
   If Sheila said that, she was lying.

4.3 Remote conditions

■ Remote conditions are used when the speaker thinks that the condition is not true and so the event is unlikely to take place:

If you really loved me, you wouldn't keep criticizing me.
I would be very surprised if she turned up now.
You could do much better if you tried harder.

The same forms are used when the condition is imaginary but untrue:

We'd have more fun if Sylvia was here.
I'd buy you an ice cream if I had my purse with me.

■ Most remote conditions use the following tenses:

Main clause: would/should + base form
If clause: simple past tense

For the difference between would and should, see (⟴ **VERBS 1, 3.5 & 3.6**). The main clause can also contain the past tense of other modals (⟴ **VERBS 1, 3.2**):

If we bought a car we *could* get up to London more often.

■ In the if clause, was often changes to were; i.e. the past subjunctive can be used (⟴ **VERBS 3, 2.2**):

I wouldn't do that if I *were* you.
If she *were* my sister I'd be very cross.

■ When the event in the if clause is in the future and considered particularly unlikely, be to + the base form of the verb is often used (⟴ **VERBS 2, 3.8**):

I'd certainly accept if they *were to offer* me the job.
If she *were to agree* we'd be able to get started on the work at once.

4.4 Hypothetical conditions

■ Hypothetical conditions are remote conditions in the past; that is, the condition is definitely untrue and the event did not happen:

I would have returned the book if I'd known you needed it.
If he hadn't had a good lawyer he might have gone to prison.

■ Most hypothetical conditions use the following tenses:

Main clause: would/should + have + past participle
if clause: past perfect tense, i.e. had + past participle

For the difference between would and should, see **VERBS 1, 3.5 & 3.6**. The main clause can also use the past tense of other modals (⟴ **VERBS 1, 3.2**).

We *could have been* home by now if we hadn't been delayed.

4.5 Conditions with subject-auxiliary inversion

Should you change you mind, please let us know at once.
Had we known about your problems, we would have paid you earlier.

■ Conditional clauses can also be formed without *if* using subject-auxiliary inversion. This construction is rather old-fashioned and formal.

4.6 Other remote tense constructions

■ The tense system in the main clauses of remote if sentences is also used in other main clauses, such as:

I'd rather you *didn't* spit.
You'd think she'd be tired of him by now.

■ The tense system in remote if clauses is used in other subordinate clauses, such as:

I wish I *weren't* so ugly.
Rebecca acts as if she *were* some sort of queen.
Suppose there *were to be* a fire.
If only I *hadn't* thrown the letter away!

See also **Verbs 1, 3.10**.

5. Comparative Clauses

■ Comparative clauses are used to complete comparative constructions (⇨ **ADJECTIVES, 2.2; ADVERBS AND ADVERBIALS, 1.2**):

> I don't find cooking as much fun as I used to do.
> Your car goes faster than I expected (it to).
> Sharon's marks are better this year than (they were) last year.
> Their new record isn't as good as the critics have been saying.

■ Than clauses are used after comparative adjectives and adverbs. As clauses are used after so or as + an adjective or adverb, or such + a noun:

> I'm not such a fool as you seem to think (I am).

5.1 Shortening in comparative clauses

> The job's more interesting now than it used to be.
> John works just as hard as his sister (does).

■ In order to make a comparison, something must be shared by both the main clause and the than or as clause. Material shared by both clauses is generally omitted from the second:

> The mountains stretch very far. + The eye can see as far.
> → The mountains stretch as far as the eye can see.

■ The exact rules governing this kind of shortening are very complicated, but in general as much is omitted as possible:

> She can type as fast as he can dictate.
> There are more books in this library than I could ever read.

■ When a main verb other than be is shared, it can be replaced by do:

> I've worked harder today than I *did* yesterday.
> He spends as much on his car as he *does* on his children.

However, extra material is often included in the comparative clause if it helps to make the meaning clear. For instance:

> I hate Bill more than you.
> → 1. I hate Bill more than I hate you.
> → 2. I hate Bill more than you do.

5.2 Comparisons with *as if* and *as though*

> You look *as though* you've seen a ghost.
> It looked *as if* it was going to rain.

Other comparative clauses are introduced by as if or as though. The past subjunctive can be used if the speaker has serious doubts about the truth of the comparison or knows it to be untrue (⇨ **VERBS 3, 2.2**):

> You don't need to shout *as if everyone were* miles away.
> Lynn suddenly went pale, *as if she were* about to faint.

6. Noun Clauses

■ Noun clauses acts like nouns within a sentence; for instance, they can be subjects or objects of verbs (➪ **Syntax 1, 1.**):

> *What they said* **surprised me greatly.**
> **I don't know** *why I thought that.*
> **It seems** *that I've made a mistake.*

■ Nouns clauses are very common in reported speech (➪ **7.**):

> **Val said** *that she was a friend of yours.*

■ English has two main kinds of clauses that act like nouns within a sentence:

1. Nominal relative clauses, beginning with what, whatever, whichever, whoever, etc:

> **Did you find** *what you were looking for?*
> **I'll go out with** *whoever I choose.*

2. Content clauses, beginning with that (or zero), a WH- word or if:

> **He told me** *where I could find some cheap furniture.*
> **I don't believe** *(that) you really mean it.*
> **I wonder** *if Vicky's heard her results yet.*

6.1 Nominal relative clauses

■ Nominal relative clauses always stand for a 'thing' rather than a 'fact'. They are used very much as ordinary nouns; for instance, they can appear after prepositions:

> **Were you surprised** *by what she did?*
> **You can tell the news to** *whoever needs to know.*

■ When they are the subject of a verb, the verb can be singular or plural depending on whether the 'thing' is felt to be one or more:

> *What I need is* **a nice cold shower.**
> *What I need are* **some two-inch nails.**

6.2 Content clauses

■ Content clauses stand for 'facts' rather than 'things':

> **I'm not sure** *that I can help you.*
> **Do you know** *if she agrees?*

They are typically used as the objects of verbs in reported speech (➪ **7.**) but have many other uses, for instance:

– Subject: **Why it happened is a mystery to me.**

–After prepositions: **I'm not happy about what he said.**

■ Especially when they are the subject of a verb, content clauses are often moved to the end of a sentence and replaced by it (➪ **Syntax 1, 2.2**):

It's a mystery to me *why it happened.*
It is thought *that Watson has now left the country.*

■ That clauses are not used after prepositions; in a full that clause the preposition is simply left out:

They were anxious *about you.*
They were anxious *that you hadn't phoned.*

That *clauses*

■ The word that in content clauses is typically omitted: compare Relative Pronouns (⇨ **PRONOUNS AND DETERMINERS, 10.3**). There is little stylistic difference; it is common to drop that even in formal written English:

We were all happy (that) you did so well.
The company does not admit (that) the goods are faulty.

■ However, that cannot be dropped at the beginning of sentences. It is also usually retained in long, complex sentences where keeping it helps to make the grammar clear:

That they are married is known to very few people.
They know *that the man who sold it has gone bankrupt.*

Non-finite content clauses

■ The -ing form of verbs (⇨ **VERBS 3, 5.**) and the to infinitive (⇨ **VERBS 3, 4.**) are often used in the same ways as content clauses:

My hobby is collecting ancient coins.
Is it possible to get there by five?

■ The to infinitive is particularly common after WH- words when the subject is obvious. In the following pairs, the first is much more common than the second:

I'm not sure *where to sit.*
I'm not sure *where I should sit.*

I didn't know *whether to laugh or cry.*
I didn't know *whether I should laugh or cry.*

■ It is the main verb that decides what kind of content clause is possible – that clause, WH- finite clause, to infinitive or -ing form. Some verbs allow more than one type (you should be able to find this information in a good dictionary). Compare:

We believed that he was a liar. *OR* We believe him to be a liar.
We said that he was a liar. *BUT NOT* We said him to be a liar.
They told us when we should come. *OR* They told us when to come.
They said to us when we should come.
BUT NOT They said to us when to come.

See also **VERBS 1, 5.**

7. Reported Speech

■ The following examples show typical forms used in:

1. Reported statements
   They said (that) they wanted to meet you.
   They told us when the programme was starting.

2. Reported questions
   I asked her whether she had seen my glasses.
   I asked them where to park my car.

3. Reported commands
   I told him (that) he should leave at once.
   I told her not to worry.
   I told them when to leave.

4. Reported exclamations.
   I was surprised how fast the time went.
   I'm surprised what a good singer he is.

The exact form is decided by the verb (or adjective) that introduces the reported speech. For instance, in reported commands tell can be followed by both finite content clauses and to infinitives; but in reported statements it can only be followed by full clauses.

7.1 Types of reported speech

Reported statements

Most verbs introducing reported statements use full content clauses – i.e. that/WH- word + verb (⮕ **6.**) – e.g. say, announce, report, claim, think:
They announced (that) the school would be closed from Wednesday.
They did not announce when it would open again.

But there are exceptions, e.g. know, believe, expect:
We know (that) he's innocent. OR **We know him to be innocent.**

Reported questions

■ Most verbs introducing reported questions use full content clauses, e.g. ask, enquire, wonder, investigate:
He asked if I could help him.

■ If the actual question was a WH- question, the content clause is introduced by the same WH- word (⮕ **PRONOUNS AND DETERMINERS, 9.**):
'*When* did you see her?' → Bill asked (me) *when* I had seen her.
'*Why* didn't he phone?' → I wonder *why* he didn't phone.

'*What* songs do you know?'
→ She asked (him) *what* songs he knew.

■ If the actual question was a yes/no question, the conjunctions used are whether or, less formally, if:

'Can you pay soon?
→ They asked (us) *whether* we could pay soon.

'Are you Liz Harris?'
→ He asked (her) *if* she was Liz Harris.

■ Some verbs, e.g. ask, wonder, want to know, can be followed by a WH- word + to infinitive:

'How do I get to London?'
→ I wondered *how to get* to London.

'How do I contact him?'
→ I wanted to know *how to contact* him.

Reported commands

■ Most verbs introducing reported commands are followed by to infinitives, e.g. command, order:

The general ordered the army to advance.

■ Tell, instruct, and some others can also be followed by a WH- word + to infinitive:

Did she tell you *where to turn off* the motorway?
We weren't told *which books to read*.

■ Some verbs, e.g. tell, insist, require, can also be followed by a that clause with an auxiliary such as should or must:

I've told you already that you should be quiet.

Say is always followed by a that clause of this sort:

My dad said that I have to help him with the gardening tomorrow.

After some verbs the present subjunctive can be used instead of should + the base form (⇨ **Verbs 3, 2.1**):

They insist that every customer *be treated* equally.

Reported exclamations

■ Most verbs introducing reported exclamations take full clauses introduced by how or what: compare exclamations in direct speech (⇨ **Syntax 1, 5.**):

I was delighted how well it worked.
I'm amazed at what good weather we've had.

■ Many of the verbs used to introduce exclamations in direct speech such as exclaim or shout can only be followed by that clauses, e.g.:

'How well she plays!'
→ He exclaimed that she played very well.

Compare

••

Some sentences can be interpreted as both reported questions and reported exclamations:

I didn't realize how much it would cost.
= 1. **'I didn't realize what its price would be.'**
= 2. **'I didn't realize that it would cost so much.'**

••

7.2 Tenses in reported speech

Julie says that she'll be here by eight.
Mark claims that we didn't pay him enough.

Tenses after present-tense main verbs

■ When the main verb is in a present tense – that is, the simple present, present progressive, future, present perfect, etc. – the tense used in the subordinate clause is 'natural': that is, it is the tense you would expect the original speaker to use:

Main verb		*Subordinate clause*
Jim says Jim will say Jim has said	(that)	his wife drives the car every day. his wife is driving the car at present. his wife will drive the car tomorrow. his wife has driven the car many times. his wife drove the car yesterday. his wife had driven the car before him, etc.

Tenses after past-tense main verbs

■ When the main verb is in a past tense – the simple past, past progressive, past perfect, would + base form, etc – there are two different methods for choosing the tense in the subordinate clause:

– *Method 1* is governed by the actual context; that is, it is exactly the same as the method used when the main clause verb is in a present tense. Let's say that you met Anne at ten o'clock in the morning and she told you that her diary for the day was as follows:

9 a.m.   arrive at school
12 a.m.   have lunch
3.30 p.m. practise the piano

You meet a friend at 2 p.m. who asks you about Anne. You might say:

Anne said (that)	she arrived at school at nine a.m. she would have lunch at midday. she will practise the piano at three thirty.

The tenses are 'natural': Anne did arrive at 9 a.m.; she would have lunch at midday; she will practise the piano at 3.30 p.m. The future in the past (⇨ **Verbs 2, 3.10**) is used in the second example because lunch was still future when Anne spoke, but it is now in the past.

This method can use any combination of tenses:

> **My sister was saying that Hamlet will be playing here next week.**
> **They told me that Joan's already had her baby.**
> **He said that his new car will go faster than his old one did.**

– *Method 2* is governed by grammar. According to this method, a past-tense main verb is always followed by a past-tense form in the subordinate clause; the tense used in the actual speech is 'moved one step back' into the past in reported speech. For example:

present → past

> **'I *go* to school.'** → He said that he *went* to school.
> **'I *am* going to work.'** → He said that he *was* going to work.

past/perfect → past perfect

> **'He *has* gone away.'** → I said that you *had gone* away.
> **'I *came* to see you.'** → He said he *had come* to see me.

future → would/should + verb

> **'She *will* go soon.'** → They said that she *would* go soon.

Past-tense verbs in the actual speech become past perfect in reported speech, e.g. went → had gone. But in this case the simple past is often retained:

> **'We *went* to church.'**
> → **He said that they *had gone* to church.**
> → **He said that they *went* to church.**

Look at the situation in the last section. Using Method 2 we get:

Anne said (that) { she (had) arrived at school at nine a.m.
she would have lunch at midday.
she would practise the piano at three thirty.

Similarly, the other examples become:

> **My sister was saying that Hamlet would be playing here next week.**
> **They told me that Joan had already had her baby.**
> **He said that his new car would go faster than his old one did/had done.**

Method 1 v. Method 2

■ Method 1 has certain advantages over Method 2. It allows the distinction to be kept between the simple past and the present progressive:

1. **Lucy said that she has worked there for years.** (She still does.)
   Lucy said that she worked there for years. (But now she has left.)
2. **Lucy said that she had worked there for years.**

And, when the tense in the actual speech was future, Method 1 keeps the distinction between events that are now past and those that are still to happen:

1. **Harry said he would come.** (But he has not come.)
   Harry said he will come. (We expect him tomorrow.)
2. **Harry said he would come.**

■ Method 2 tends to be used if the reporter has any serious doubts about the truth of what he or she is reporting. Method 1 is preferred if the fact reported is definitely true. Compare:

> **Polly said she was playing hockey this afternoon, but I don't believe her.**
> **Polly said she's playing hockey this afternoon, so that must be her hockey stick.**
> **I told him we've won some money. Was that sensible of me?**
> **I told him we'd won some money just to make him jealous.**

■ Changes to some words are predictable in reported speech:

Direct speech		*Reported speech*
now	→	**then, at that time, before…**
today	→	**on that day**
yesterday	→	**the day before**
tomorrow	→	**the next day, the day after**
next week	→	**the following week**
last week	→	**the week before**
a year ago	→	**the year before**
here	→	**there**
this	→	**that**

7.3 Modals in reported speech

■ The past-tense forms of the modals do not in general act as true past tenses (⇨ **VERBS 1, 3.**). However, reported speech is an exception:

> **'You may go.'** → **They said that I might go.**
> **'Can you help me?'** → **I asked whether he could help me.**

■ Would, could, should, ought to and modal need do not usually have past tenses (⇨ **VERBS 1, 3.7 & 3.8**). But in reported speech they can act as their own past tenses:

> **'You ought to try harder.'**
> → **They said that he ought to try harder.**
> **'Do I have to go?'** → **She asked whether she need go.**

■ In reported speech, must can act as its own past tense, or be replaced by had to (when it means have to):

> **'I must stay at home.'**
> → **I told her that I must stay at home.**
> → **I told her that I had to stay at home.**

7.4 Omission of *that*

■ That can be omitted after common verbs of saying and thinking, e.g. say, think, tell:

He said (that) he liked her.
He told her (that) he was getting married.

■ That is not usually omitted in more formal style, and is necessary after certain verbs, e.g. reply:

They replied that it would be difficult.

8. Punctuation

■ The comma is used:

– to separate words in a list:

We went to Italy, France, Spain and Portugal.
He was tall, dark and handsome.

▶ Note in British English, no comma is used before the final **and**.

– to separate off sentence adverbials:

I am, however, very happy with the decision.

– to separate off non-defining relative clauses:

Her son, who is in the army, lives in London.

– to separate off thousands:

5,354

▶ Note the comma is *not* used before reported speech clauses:

He said that he was a spy.

■ The colon is used:

– to introduce an explanation:

The solution is obvious: he killed her while the others were out in the garden.

– to introduce a list:

You will need the following: a piece of paper, some pens and a paper clip.

– to introduce quotations:

As Thatcher once said: 'There is no alternative'.

■ The semi-colon is used:

– between grammatically independent sentences when the ideas are closely connected:

Half the class played tennis; the other half went swimming.

■ The full-stop (or period in American English) is used:

– between grammatically independent sentences:

He opened the door. The dog came rushing in.

– to separate off decimal places:

4.7849

■ Quotation marks/inverted commas are used:

– to quote direct speech:

'Hello', he shouted.

– to indicate titles:

He is currently starring in 'The Mousetrap'.

– to draw attention to a particular word, either because of unusual usage, or because the word itself is being commented on:

In 'comb', the 'b' is not pronounced.

■ The apostrophe is used:

– to form the possessive:

Andrew's car.

– in contracted forms:

I'll see you later.

– with words which do not usually have plurals (such as numbers and letters):

It is spelt with two r's.

Guide to Spelling and Pronunciation

A

[æ] is the normal pronunciation of **a**
e.g. Dad, hat.

[ɑ:] is the received British pronunciation of **a** in some
words e.g. after, bath.
Many English speakers and most Americans use
[æ] here also.

[ə] is the usual pronunciation in an unstressed vowel
e.g. arrive [əˈraɪv], banana [bəˈnɑ:nə].

al (especially at the beginning of a word) and **all**
are usually pronounced [ɔ:l]
e.g. fall, hall, always, talk.

ar is usually pronounced [ɑ:]
e.g. dark, market BUT NOTICE warn [wɔ:n].

ai, **ay**, or an **a** followed by a consonant and an **e**
usually represent [eɪ]
e.g. wait, day, make BUT NOTICE Friday [ˈfraɪdɪ].

are and **air** at the end of a word are usually pronounced [eə]
e.g. care, prepare, fair, stairs.

C

[k] is the usual pronunciation before the letters **a, o, r**
and **u**
e.g. cat, cow, cross, cut.

[s] is the usual pronunciation before the letters **e, i**
and **y**
e.g. certainly, cinema, bicycle.

ch is usually pronounced [tʃ]
e.g. cheese, catch BUT NOTICE machine [məˈʃi:n],
chemist [ˈkemɪst].

E

[e] is the usual pronunciation of **e** before consonants
e.g. metal, pet.

[ə] is sometimes used when **e** is unstressed, especially at
the end of a word
e.g. player [ˈpleɪəʳ].

[ɪ] is also used when e is unstressed, especially at the beginning of a word
e.g. decide [dɪ'saɪd], pocket ['pɒkɪt].

ea is most often pronounced [iː]
e.g. heat [hiːt], peace [piːs] BUT NOTICE head [hed], break [breɪk].

ear also varies in pronunciation
e.g. near [nɪəʳ], early ['ɜːlɪ], heart [hɑːt], bear [beəʳ].

ee is usually pronounced [iː] e.g. see, meet.

er is usually pronounced [ɜː], or [ə] in an unstressed syllable e.g. term [tɜːm], perhaps [pə'hæps].

ew is usually pronounced [uː] or [juː]
e.g. flew [fluː], few [fjuː] BUT NOTICE sew [səʊ].

-(ed) (added to regular verbs to form the past tense and past participle) is pronounced:
–[t] if the base form ends in [f, k, p, s, ʃ, tʃ, θ]
e.g. cooked [kʊkt], finished ['fɪnɪʃt].
–[d] if the base form ends in [b, ð, dʒ, g, l, m, n, ŋ, v, z, ʒ] or a vowel
e.g. loved [lʌvd], cried [kraɪd].
–[ɪd] if the if the base form ends in [d] or [t]
e.g. avoided [ə'vɔɪdɪd].

G

[g] is the usual pronunciation of **g**
e.g. get, give, bag.
However before **e** or **i** it is sometimes pronounced [dʒ]
e.g. generally, page, engine.

H

[h] is the usual pronunciation of **h**
e.g. hat, heavy,
but there are a few words where the **h** is not pronounced
e.g. hour [aʊəʳ].

I

[ɪ] is the most common pronunciation of **i**
e.g. hit, fill, milk.

[aɪ] is sometimes used when **i** is followed by a consonant and an **e**, or in the spelling **igh** e.g. nice, idea, night.

ie is usually pronounced [iː]
e.g. field, piece.

ir is usually pronounced [ɜː]
e.g. dirty, third.

J

[dʒ] is the pronunciation of **j**
e.g. job, just.

L

[l]   is the pronunciation of **l**.
Note that in some words this sound may make up
a syllable
e.g. leg, letter, little, metal.

There are a few words where **l** is not pronounced
e.g. half [hɑːf], walk [wɔːk], could [kʊd].

N

[n]   is the usual pronunciation of **n**.
Note that in some words this sound may make up a syllable
e.g. name, nine, hand, curtain.

[ŋ]   is the usual pronunciation before **c**, **k** and **g**
e.g. uncle, hang, interesting, pink.

O

[ɒ]   is the normal pronunciation of **o** when it is followed by a
single consonant, a double consonant, and most combinations
of two consonants
e.g. hot, coffee, cost.

[əʊ] is also common, especially when **o** is followed by a consonant
and an **e** e.g. hole, stone, hotel, most BUT NOTICE done [dʌn],
move [muːv].

[ə]   is the pronunciation of **o** in unstressed syllables
e.g. collect [kə'lekt], tomato [tə'mɑːtəʊ].

oa is usually pronounced [əʊ]
e.g. boat, loaf.

oi, oy is usually pronounced [ɔɪ]
e.g. toy, voice.

or is usually pronounced [ɔː]
> e.g. **more, sort** BUT NOTICE **lorry** [ˈlɒrɪ], **orange** [ˈɒrɪndʒ].

oo is sometimes pronounced [uː] and sometimes [ʊ]
> e.g. **loose** [luːs], **look** [lʊk] BUT NOTICE **blood** [blʌd].

ou, ow are commonly pronounced [aʊ]
> e.g. **loud, sound, cow, town.**

ow can also be pronounced [əʊ]
> e.g. **low, know.**

and **ou** can also represent various other sounds,
> e.g. **soup** [suːp], **touch** [tʌtʃ].

P

[p] is the usual pronunciation of **p**
> e.g. **pen** [pen], **happy** [ˈhæpɪ].

ph is pronounced [f]
> e.g. **phone** [fəʊn], **photograph** [ˈfəʊtəɡrɑːf].

Q

[kw] is the pronunciation of q, which is always followed
> by the letter **u**
> e.g. **question, quick.**

R

[r] is the pronunciation of **r** in British Received Pronunciation
only when it is followed by a vowel. In American English **r** is
always pronounced.
Note that the pronunciation of vowels usually changes
before **r**; this is explained at **a, e, i, o** and **u**
> e.g. **narrow, various,** BUT **farm** [fɑːm], **storm** [stɔːm].

r at the end of a word is only pronounced if the the
next word begins with a vowel. The symbol [ʳ] is used to
indicate this
> e.g. **driver** [ˈdraɪvəʳ], **stare** [steəʳ], but **four of them** [ˈfɔrəvðəm].

S

[s] is the pronunciation of **s** when it is the first letter of a
> word, and when it is followed by **c, k, p** and **t** or another **s**
> e.g. **six, escape, ask, especially, mistake, miss.**
In other cases **s** is sometimes pronounced [s] and
sometimes [z]
> e.g. **season** [ˈsiːzn], **upstairs** [ʌpˈsteəz], **asleep** [əˈsliːp].

se at the end of word is usually pronounced [z]
e.g. rose.

sh is pronounced [ʃ] e.g. dish, fashion.

T

[t] is the normal pronunciation of **t**
e.g. toast, tray
but in the middle of some words in front of a vowel
it is pronounced [tʃ] or [ʃ]
e.g. question ['kwestʃən], patient ['peɪʃnt].

th is usually pronounced [θ] at the beginning or the end
of a word
e.g. thank, thin, bath.

[ð] is the pronunciation of th in determiners like this [ðɪs],
the [ðiː, ðə], there [ðeəʳ] and than [ðæn]. In the middle of
words, both [θ and [ð] occur
e.g. nothing ['nʌθɪŋ], mother ['mʌðəʳ]

U

[ʌ] is the most common pronunciation of **u**
e.g. funny, under.

[uː, juː] are also common pronunciations, especially when **u**
is followed by **e** or by a consonant and **e**
e.g. music ['mjuːzɪk], truth [truːθ], blue [bluː] huge [hjuːdʒ].

Other possible pronunciations are [ʊ], especially before **l** and **sh,**
and [ə] in unstressed syllables
e.g. pull [pʊl], push [pʊʃ], put [pʊt], suppose [sə'pəʊz].

ur is usually pronounced [ɜː], or [ə] in unstressed syllables
e.g. curtain ['kɜːtn], surprise [sə'praɪz].

W

[w] is the pronunciation of **w**
e.g. wet.

wr is pronounced [r] as in wrong [rɒŋ].

X

[ks] is the normal pronunciation of **x**
e.g. taxi ['tæksɪ]
but **ex** is pronounced [ɪgz] at the beginning of some words

when a stressed vowel follows
e.g. **example** [ɪgˈzɑːmpl].

Y

[j]   is the pronunciation of **y** before a vowel
e.g. **yes** [jes].

[aɪ, ɪ] are alternative pronounciations of **y** as a stressed
vowel sound.

[ɪ]   is the pronunciation of **y** as an unstressed final syllable
e.g. **mystery** [ˈmɪstərɪ], **cry** [kraɪ], **ugly** [ˈʌglɪ].

Glossary

■ Active

The subject of an active verb form is the person or thing that carries out the action of the verb.

> *S   V   O*
> **She killed him.**

This should be contrasted with the passive verb form (see below), where the subject is the person or thing affected by the action of the verb.

■ Adjective

Although many grammar books say that an adjective is 'a word that indicates a quality of the person or thing referred to by a noun', it is more helpful to describe it according to its form and position in a sentence. In the Slavonic languages, for example, adjectives can be recognized immediately by their form, but in English there are only a few characteristic endings, e.g. -able, -ish and -ous, and nouns can act freely as adjectives, since no special inflection is necessary. In addition, unlike most Indo-European languages, English does not show case, number or gender in its adjectives. For this reason, position is a better guide. The most characteristic position is between a determiner and a noun:

> **This *old* house.**
> **A *new* car.**

Adjectives can also follow **be** and other linking verbs, e.g. **seem, get, become, appear**. Since nouns can also fill this position, we can check whether the word is an adjective by inserting the word **very**:

> **They are *very* useless.** = adjective
> *NOT* **They are *very* teachers.** = noun

■ Adverb

Many grammar books say that adverbs modify (that is, give more information about) verbs:

> **She ran *quickly.***

or adjectives:

> ***Very* good.**

However, they are most honestly described as words that do not fit into other groups. They can be partly described according to form, position and function:

Form – many end in **-ly**, but the majority have no special form (both **very** and **quickly** are adverbs).

Position – they can occur in three positions:
– before the subject:

Then he arrived.

– between subject and verb:

He *then* said.

– after an intransitive verb, object or complement:

He left *quickly*.

▶ Note you can never say in English 'He paid quickly the money'.

Function: they can modify verbs:

She sat *quietly*.

adjectives:

Very good.

nouns:

Rather a mess.

and pronouns:

Virtually nothing.

■ Adverbial

The adverbial provides information about place, time, manner, circumstances, etc. In any English sentence, the subject and verb are normally obligatory and fixed in position, but the adverbial is a mobile optional extra:

I *usually* drink beer. *NOT* I usually beer.
Usually I drink beer. *NOT* Usually drink beer.
I drink beer, *usually.*

The key word to describe adverbials is 'several' because:
– there can be several in one clause.
– they can take several forms.
– they can be in several positions in one clause.

■ Affirmative

⇨ **Non-Affirmative**

■ Auxiliary

Since they 'help' to complete the meaning of the full verb, there are two very distinct but small groups of verbs in English which are called 'auxiliaries'. Both cause problems for foreign learners when they combine to produce such forms as:

He might have been being examined.

The two groups are:
– the three primary auxiliaries **be**, **do** and **have**, which are used to form the 12 tenses and their negative, passive and question forms:

Hasn't she been asked? Didn't he know?

– the nine 'modal' auxiliaries (⇨ **VERBS 1, 3.**).

■ Case

Case is what we call the change in the form of a noun, adjective, participle or pronoun that shows its relationship to another word, e.g. in German *der* **Mann** becomes *den* **Mann** to show, among other things, that it is the direct object of a verb. A thousand years ago English was like German or Russian: almost all nouns, adjectives and pronouns had many different endings to show their function in a sentence. Modern English is very different. The only words which still change their form to show their function are pronouns:

**I → me . he → him . she → her . we → us . they → them
who → whom**

You should use **me**, **him**, etc under the following conditions:

– in the object position:

Can you see *him*?

– after prepositions:

Give it to *me*, right now!

– as the complement of **be** (in spoken English):

It's *me*.

– after **as** and **than** in comparative constructions (in spoken English):

She's cleverer than *me*.

– when a pronoun is joined by **and** to another word (in spoken English):

Who's coming? Jim and *me*.

■ Clause

A clause is a group of words that usually includes a subject and a finite or non-finite verb, forming a sentence or part of a sentence, e.g. the sentences below all consist of two clauses, separated by a comma:

Although I felt ill, I went out.
Although feeling ill, I went out.
Going out with wet hair, I caught a chill.
If possible, don't go out.

Clauses are usually divided into two types:

– *Subordinate*

A subordinate clause begins with a conjunction or participle (e.g. **because, since, although, walking, going**) and *must* be used with a main clause to complete its meaning:

Although I felt ill, ...

– *Main*

A main clause does not need another clause to complete its meaning and so can be used on its own:

I went out.

■ Cleft Sentences

Cleft sentences are used to draw particular attention to the subject or the object by using a structure beginning with it or **what**:

John hit Dave. → **It was John who hit Dave.** (focus on subject)

→ **It was Dave that John hit.** (focus on object)

I like the colour. → **What I like is the colour.**

→ **It's the colour I like.** (focus on object)

■ Comparative

The forms used in a language to compare two sets of things are called the 'comparative'. In English we can make comparisons with adjectives and adverbs, using either -er or the adverb **more**. The choice of comparative form depends on the length of the word:

long → **longer**
difficult → **more difficult**

■ Complement

The complement provides extra information about the subject or object of a sentence. It completes the meaning of certain verbs (be, become, seem) and structures:

He became *a teacher.* (telling more about the subject he)

The P.M. made him *a minister.* (telling more about the direct object him)

A good dictionary will indicate when a complement is necessary or possible.

■ Complementation

Complementation describes the word which completes the meaning of a phrase and clause and determines its grammatical relationship with the following phrases or clauses. This mainly affects verbs and adjectives:

Look *at* these pictures.
The heat made me *sleepy.*
I've decided *to* go.
I enjoy play*ing* tennis.
It's difficult *to* play.
She's good *at* maths.

Since the patterns are very varied and difficult to remember, read the main text very carefully.

■ Conjunction

A 'conjunction' is a word which joins two clauses, phrases or words. There are two kinds:

– *Coordinating*: these join any two equal elements (e.g. and, but, or):

Bread *and* butter.
I opened the door, *but* saw nothing.

– *Subordinating*: these join only clauses, not phrases or individual words (e.g. that, what, when). A clause beginning with such a conjunction is called a subordinate clause and cannot be used alone:

***After/before/when* I left, I locked the door.**

■ Continuous

⟹ **PROGRESSIVE**

■ Contraction

In spoken English the word not and the verbs be, have, will, shall and would can be used in a shortened or 'contracted' form:

I can't do it ⹁ I've found it ⹁ I'd/I'll go ⹁ I shan't tell

■ Countability

'Countability', a very important part of the grammar of the noun phrase, is a way of grouping nouns into those which can or cannot be counted:

5 cats BUT NOT **5 sands.**

Those which take a plural can be counted and used with a/the and are called 'countable':

dog, cat, bird are 'countable'
justice, truth, love are 'uncountable'

▶ Note that a noun which is countable in your language may not be in English, so always check your dictionary.

■ Declarative

The declarative is used for making statements. The basic word order is

$S + V + O$

but study the main text for other common patterns.

■ Determiner

A determiner is one of a large group of very common words whose function is to 'determine' or limit what the following noun phrase can refer to:

the = 'definite'
a = 'indefinite'
some = 'part of a whole'

They usually come at the beginning of a noun phrase and always before any adjective, but the choice and order of determiner(s) depend on both the type of noun and determiner.

■ Direct Object

⇨ **OBJECT**

■ Extraposition

This term is used to describe the shifting of a subject clause to the end of a sentence and its replacement by the word **it**. This is to avoid beginning a sentence with a **to-** clause (or sometimes an **-ing** clause), which is felt to be awkward, especially in spoken English:

To meet you is nice. → **It's nice to meet you.**
Going by bus to work then walking all the way across town in the rain is tiresome. → **It's tiresome going...**

■ Finite

In English all verbs except the modal auxiliaries can have two forms: finite and non-finite.

– *Finite* (**know/knows/knew**) verb forms usually have a subject, show tense and can form a sentence.

– *Non-finite* verb forms (infinitive, **-ing**, **-ed**) have no subject and cannot form a sentence. They are used both to form finite complex tenses and in complementation:

Discovering **the key, I went in.** (non-finite)
I want *to know.* (non-finite)
She *was walking.* (finite + non-finite = finite)

■ Imperative

The 'imperative' is the name we give to the command form of the verb. Unlike most languages, English has no special imperative inflection – we simply use the base form (the form you find in the dictionary). Sometimes the auxiliary **do** or the pronoun **you** are added for negation or emphasis:

Look!
Do shut up!
You listen to me, young man!

▶ Note that this is the only sentence type in English where the subject can be omitted.

■ Impersonal Verbs

Impersonal verbs are those which follow the subject **it**. They are commonly used when talking about the weather or time:

> **It's raining.**
> **It's hot and sunny.**
> **It's half past six.**

■ Indirect Object

⇨ **OBJECT**

■ Infinitive

This is one of the non-finite verb forms in English. It has no special inflection, but is usually divided into the 'bare' infinitive or base form (**go**) and the **to**-infinitive (**to go**), which has eight complex forms (see the main text for details). There are many uses for both the bare infinitive and **to** infinitive which should be investigated in the main text.

■ Inflection

When we change the ending of a word to show its function in a sentence, we call these changes 'inflections'. Modern English is unique among the Indo-European languages in having very few inflections: -es, -ing, -ed, -er, -est.

■ Interrogative

The interrogative is used for asking questions. The basic word order is

$$AUX + S + V$$

but study the main text for other common patterns.

■ Intransitive

An intransitive verb is one that is not followed by a direct object:

> **listen   depend   look**

If intransitive verbs are followed by an object, the object is indirect and preceded by a preposition:

> **listen to   depend on   look at**

Intransitive verbs cannot be used in the passive.

■ Linking Verbs

Linking verbs are verbs which mainly link the subject to its noun or adjective complement or to an adverbial. When the complement is a noun, it and the subject refer to the same person or thing, but compare:

He became a teacher (*He* = teacher)
He knew the teacher (*He* ≠ teacher)

Among the most common linking verbs are:

appear	be	become
feel	get	grow
look	seem	smell
sound	taste	turn

■ Modal Auxiliaries

There are nine modal auxiliaries: can, could, may, might, must, shall, should, will, would. A modal auxiliary is one which expresses an attitude to or feeling about a situation, e.g. possibility (**can**), likelihood (**might**), obligation (**must**), etc. Since this very important group is grammatically different from other verbs and has a complex and subtle range of meanings, you should study the relevant section very carefully.

■ Non-Affirmative

Non-affirmative forms refer to those determiners, pronouns and adverbs which are used in negative and semi-negative sentences, such as **any, much, yet** and **either**.

■ Non-Finite

⇨ Finite

■ Noun

Try not to think of a noun as the 'name' of somebody or something because it will not really help you to understand English grammar. As with adjectives or adverbs, think of nouns in terms of position, function and form.

Unlike many languages English does not often show a noun by its form:

arrival = noun *BUT* **cultural** = adjective
harden = verb *BUT* **garden** = noun.

Even the ending -s is not completely reliable:

Houses with gardens. (plural)
He gardens every weekend. (verb inflection)

The best tests are position and function. Nouns are very often preceded by determiners and adjectives, and can be the subject, object and complement of a clause, or the object of a preposition. For more information on the different types of noun consult the main text.

■ Object

In grammar we call the 'direct' object the person or thing affected by the action of the verb and the 'indirect' object the receiver of the action:

Give the book to your sister.
        Od   *Oi*

▶ Note if the indirect object is a pronoun, it must *always* precede the direct object:

Give her the book.
    Oi   *Od*

Both kinds of object are either noun phrases or noun clauses, and usually follow the verb, unless we wish to emphasize them by moving them to the beginning of the clause:

I'll give it to him. (unemphatic)
Him I'll give this one, but that one I'll save. (emphatic)

▶ Note that since in English only the personal pronouns change to show that they are acting as direct or indirect objects, it is not useful to call the direct object the 'accusative case' or the indirect object the 'dative case'.

■ Object Complement

⇨ COMPLEMENT

■ Participle

A participle is one of the non-finite forms of the English verb, ending in -ing (the present participle) or -ed (the past participle) and used in the verb phrase:

I am going . I have walked

▶ Note that there are about 250 verbs in English which have irregular past participles, many ending in -t or -n. The main text contains a list of the most common ones.

In addition, although many present and past participles can act as adjectives, there are some adjectives ending in -ed that look like participles but which are not based on verbs, e.g.:

You are so talented. *NOT* **to talent**
She came uninvited. *NOT* **to uninvite**

■ Passive

In English, a compound verb form made up of one of the forms of be (and often get) and the -ed participle is called the 'passive':

She was/got killed

However, the passive is not, strictly speaking, part of the grammar of the verb (⇨ -ing, -ed, -s), but one of the ways of giving special emphasis or meaning to a clause or part of it. If you want to emphasize the person or thing affected by an action (usually the direct object), you make that person or thing the subject of a passive construction:

The man in the dark suit told me that...
(= the person who told me is more important)
I have been told that...
(= who told me is unimportant)

▶ Note that:
– Passive forms are freely used in the spoken language and are *not* 'bookish'.

– Active and passive sentences are *not* just different ways of saying the same thing.

■ Perfect

This is the name we use to describe the verb form composed of have + -ed participle. It is used in a past, present or future framework to indicate the time preceding *and* still relevant to the time shown by the auxiliary:

She has arrived. (= some time before now and is now present)

▶ Note that even if a similar form exists in your language, its uses are probably different from English and should be checked carefully, since this tense can be difficult to use properly.

■ Phrasal Verb

A phrasal verb is often called a 'multi-word verb', which shows clearly that it is a verb made up of two or three words, usually a fairly common verb + one or two of nearly 50 words that function as adverbs, prepositions or both:

get up ⸱ fall down ⸱ put up with.

The problem with such verbs is not only that the new meaning created cannot usually be guessed from the constituent words but also that there may be two or more unrelated meanings:

put → **put up new curtains** (= hang)
    → **put up a guest** (= give a guest a bed for the night)
    → **put up with** (= endure)

In addition, even though their meanings seem to be the same as single-word verbs, they are usually more informal in style.

■ Phrase

Any sentence may be divided for analysis into smaller groups of words which are considered to belong together. These smaller groups are called 'phrases', e.g. the following sentence:

'The weather in Wales has been really awful for a week now.'

can be divided as follows:

The weather in Wales = noun phrase (since the central word is a noun)

has been = verb phrase

really awful = adjective phrase (since the central word is an adjective)

for a week now = adverb phrase (since the central word is an adverb)

■ Plural

In grammar we use the word 'plural' to describe the form of a noun, verb or pronoun which refers to more than one person or thing. In many languages these forms can be complex and varied, but in English forming the plural is relatively simple, since only nouns, this/that, the verb be and certain reflexive pronouns show the plural:

dogs ⸱ these/those ⸱ are/were ⸱ ourselves/themselves

■ Possessive

'Possessive' is the term we use for the small group of words which show who 'possesses/owns/has/is related to' the noun they refer to. In English there are two kinds:

– those which are determiners and stand before nouns:

my/your/his/her/its/our/their friend

– those which are pronouns and stand alone:

It is mine/yours/hers/his/ours/theirs

▶ Note that there is no pronoun its.

■ Preposition

Prepositions are a large fixed group of words (e.g. in, from, out of, by means of) used before nouns, pronouns, and wh- and -ing clauses to show place, position, time, method, etc. They are also used as complements of verbs, adjectives and occasionally nouns (a good dictionary will tell you):

good at ⸱ depend on

▶ Note that they can never be followed by:

– a that clause:

NOT **I insisted on that she went.**

– a to infinitive

NOT **I insisted on to meet him.**

– the subject form of the personal pronouns:

NOT **Are you interested in he?**

■ Progressive

The 'progressive' is a compound verb form made up of a form of **be** and the **-ing** participle. It is sometimes called the 'continuous'. Its essential function is to limit the time established by the verb **be** (past, present or future):

She sings beautifully. (= this is always true)
She's singing beautifully. (= refers only to the time of speaking)

■ Pronoun

As its name suggests, a pronoun is a word we use in place of a noun or noun phrase:

The man knows *the woman*. → **He knows *her*.**

The forms of these words are varied and should be checked in the appropriate section of the main text.

▶ Note that five of the personal pronouns (those usually referring to human beings) are unusual in English because they always show 'case':

I → **me ▲ he** → **him ▲ she** → **her ▲ we** → **us ▲ they** → **them**

■ Quantifiers

These are the five groups of determiners and pronouns in English we use to express quantity or amount, e.g. **several, some, lots**.

■ Reflexive

We use this term to describe a word which shows that the action of the verb is performed on its subject:

I've cut *myself*.

Reflexive pronouns are formed by adding **-self** (singular) and **-selves** (plural) to:

– the possessive:
   myself/yourself/ourselves/yourselves
– the direct object form:
   her-/him-/itself; themselves
– 'one':
   oneself

■ Relative

We use this term to describe that group of words known as relative pronouns and adverbs which refer to an earlier noun, clause or sentence:

The woman *who* lives across the street.
That was the year *when* they invaded the country.

▶ Note that in English, unlike other European languages, the choice of relative pronoun is *not* determined by gender. For more information on the choice of pronoun, check the main text.

■ Reported

When in English we wish to report other people's or our own words or thoughts, a complex system of tense, adverb, pronoun and determiner changes is required, known as 'backshift':

'Are you enjoying yourself?' → **She asked if I was enjoying myself.**

All these changes are called reported (or sometimes 'indirect') speech, thoughts, questions, etc. They are exceptionally complex and should be studied carefully.

■ Semi-modals

There are four verbs in English (**ought to, used to, need** and **dare**) which belong to the modal group in meaning, but have grammatical features which the other modals do not have:

She needs to know.
→ **She need not know.** (position of **not**; **do** is not used)
I dared to go.
→ **How dare you!** (**do** is not used)
You ought to stop.
→ **Ought you to do that?** (**do** is not used)
I used to know.
→ **I used not to know.** (position of **not**; **did** is not used)

Since they belong to both modal and non-modal verbs, they are called 'semi-modals'.

■ Sentence

If a group of words includes a subject and a finite verb, we usually call it a 'sentence'. A sentence can be described according to the number of clauses it contains:

– *Simple*: one subject and one finite verb (we could also call it a 'main clause').
– *Compound*: when the sentence contains more than one clause and the clauses are joined by such words as **and, or, but, so** or **then**.
– *Complex*: one or more subordinate clauses and a main clause.

■ Subject

In every English sentence there must be a verb and almost always a subject (except in imperatives), so we call the subject one of the two essential elements of a sentence. It usually precedes the verb and cannot be moved freely like the adverbial. The subject names who or what does or is affected by the action described by the verb:

He **teaches English.** = he does the action

He **is taught English.** = he is affected by the action

■ Subject Complement

⇨ COMPLEMENT

■ Subjunctive

In grammar we call the special form of a verb that expresses a wish, possibility, condition, etc the 'subjunctive'. Unlike many other European languages, modern English cannot really be said to have a subjunctive system, since it can be and usually is replaced by other tenses or modals and occurs in only two forms:

I/(s)he were   **(s)he do**

When it does occur, it marks the speaker as very formal:

'I demand that he go.' is usually replaced by **'I demand that he should go.'**

■ Subordinate

⇨ CLAUSE

■ Superlative

The superlative is used to say that a person or thing has qualities which exceed others in a group of two or more. In English, we can use the superlative with both adjectives and adverbs. It is formed by adding either -est or the adverb most, and by placing the before the adjective or adverb. The choice of superlative form depends on the length of the word:

long → **the longest**

difficult → **the most difficult**

■ Syntax

Syntax deals with the ways in which words go together to form clauses and sentences, e.g. statements, negatives, questions, commands.

■ Tag Questions

These are very short positive or negative questions added on to statements, usually to ask for confirmation:

You're coming, *aren't you?*

They can also express disbelief, surprise or sarcasm:

You're not serious, *are you?*

Although they consist only of a subject and an auxiliary verb, their formation and use can be confusing, so they should be studied carefully in the main text.

■ Tense

Do not confuse 'time' and 'tense': 'time' is a philosophical concept we apply to the physical world, whereas 'tense' is what most languages use to represent the speaker's way of looking at time by changing the shape of the verb (by inflections).

Although we can talk of past, present and future 'time' we can talk of only past and present 'tenses' in English, because there is no inflection to show future tense. If you consult the text, you will see there are many ways to express future time, but no future tense.

■ Thematic Fronting

A clause may be moved to the front of a sentence to give it special emphasis. This is known as 'thematic fronting':

That money I owe you, can I give it to you tomorrow?

■ Transitive

A transitive verb is one that is followed by a direct object:

drive (a car) ▪ smoke (a pipe) ▪ answer (a question)

Some transitive verbs are always followed by a direct object:

like ▪ say

Others, like drive, smoke and answer can sometimes be used without an object (see **INTRANSITIVE** above).

■ Uncountable

⇨ **COUNTABILITY**

■ Verbs

In Russian a single adverbial can constitute a sentence. In English this is impossible. We can omit all the elements of a sentence, even the subject (e.g. shut up!), but no sentence exists without a verb. Do not confuse this with verbless non-finite clauses, such as 'if possible'. There are two important things to remember about the English verb:

1. The place of the verb in the sentence is usually filled by the 'verb phrase', so-called because it can comprise up to six words:

I might not have been being followed.

2. Verbs are divided into three groups:

– 'Full' or 'main' verbs, e.g. work, go, live.
– The three 'auxiliary' verbs, e.g. be, do, have.
– The nine 'modal' verbs, e.g. can, may, will.

■ Wh- Words

The words who(m), whose, what, which, where, when, why and how are so common and important in English grammar that they are called the wh- words. Their main characteristic is that they stand in initial position in a clause whether they are:

– questions:

Who are you?

– relative:

I know the woman *who* lives there.

– subordinating:

I don't know *when* he's coming.

Their main function is to ask about:

– the subject:

Who is he?

– object:

Who(m) did you see?

– complement:

What will you call the baby?

– adverbial:

When do they open?

Index

Impression MAME IMPRIMEURS, Tours.
Dépôt légal : octobre 1993 - N° 30809 - N° éditeur 17654
Imprimé en France *(Printed in France)* - 406003 octobre 1993